D0338397

THE LITTLE BOOK

OF
HEDGE FUNDS

Little Book Big Profits Series

In the *Little Book Big Profits* series, the brightest icons in the financial world write on topics that range from tried-and-true investment strategies to tomorrow's new trends. Each book offers a unique perspective on investing, allowing the reader to pick and choose from the very best in investment advice today.

Books in the *Little Book Big Profits* series include:

THE LITTLE BOOK

OF

HEDGE FUNDS

What You Need to Know About

Hedge Funds but the Managers

Won't Tell You

ANTHONY SCARAMUCCI

FOREWORD BY
NOURIEL ROUBINI

WILEY

John Wiley & Sons, Inc.

Published by John Wiley & Sons, Inc., Hoboken, New Jersey.
Published simultaneously in Canada.

For general information on our other products and services or for technical support, please contact our Customer Care Department within the United States at (800) 762-2974, outside the United States at (317) 572-3993 or fax (317) 572-4002.

Wiley also publishes its books in a variety of electronic formats. Some content that appears in print may not be available in electronic books. For more information about Wiley products, visit our web site at www.wiley.com.

Library of Congress Cataloging-in-Publication Data:

Scaramucci, Anthony.
     The little book of hedge funds : what you need to know about hedge funds but the managers won't tell you / Anthony Scaramucci. — 1
        pages cm.—(Little book big profits series)
     ISBN 978-1-118-09967-4 (hardback); ISBN 978-1-118-23707-6 (ebk);
     ISBN 978-1-118-22373-4 (ebk); ISBN 978-1-118-26204-7 (ebk)
        1. Hedge funds. I. Title.
   HG4530.S363 2012
   332.64'524—dc23

                                                                        2012005564

Printed in the United States of America
10 9 8 7 6 5 4 3 2 1

To my great kids,
Alexander, Amelia, and Anthony.
I am so grateful that we are a
part of each other's journey, and
I love the three of you with all of my heart.

Contents

Foreword

———————— ❧ ————————

In 1972 Woody Allen filmed the funny movie *Everything You Always Wanted to Know about Sex But Were Afraid to Ask*. It has taken 40 years, but now finally Anthony Scaramucci has written the perfect and comprehensive manual on *Everything You Always Wanted to Know about Hedge Funds But Were Afraid to Ask*.

Using the layman's language and a wit that at times parallels that of Woody Allen's comic genius as Anthony is a man who is as funny as he is smart. He provides the perfect primer on the esoteric world of hedge funds and their investment strategies. And being an insider who knows about hedge funds as much as anyone can—by running a leading fund of hedge funds—Anthony can reveal in simple but clear and still profound terms the explanation of exotic terms such as *alpha*, *absolute returns*, *shorting*, *hedging*, *leverage*, and *two-and-twenty*. It is a true insider's guide to hedge funds.

In the process he discusses many important open and controversial issues. Is there true alpha? My answer is a partial yes, as there are a number of hedge fund managers who can provide superior uncorrelated absolute returns even if many others are just mimicking beta or do not have superior investment skills. So it does take a lot of work to pick the right managers, and that is the challenging role that funds of hedge fund can and should play.

Why has the industry become so big? Because in a world of low returns on traditional investments as zero policy rates are now the norm, there is a huge demand for higher absolute returns. And, until 2008, those returns were higher than those on traditional passive or even active long-only strategies. Given the massive losses that the industry faced in 2008 and 2009, an open question is whether those higher returns were based on superior skills or rather leveraged beta. The jury is still out, but there are certainly some managers who are consistently providing alpha (if at a steep set of fees).

Why are hedge funds interesting to institutional investors? Because in a world where returns on traditional investments are low and pension funds have large unfunded liabilities, the search for the holy grail of alpha can diversify risk and provide superior returns. However, we also know that when risk is off rather than on—when tail risk implies high risk aversion—all risky assets become perfectly correlated and there is nowhere to hide, even among hedge funds. So, again, finding better managers becomes key.

Finally, what is the future of the hedge fund industry? Most likely a shake-up: thousands of smaller and under-performing funds have disappeared in the past few years while the more successful players are consolidating and becoming bigger. But then the issue remains of whether successful funds can maintain alpha returns when they become so large that they can move markets or they run out of successful trading ideas.

There are thus still many questions on the present and the future of the hedge fund industry. But no one else is as good as Anthony in providing a clear and yet rigorous introduction to this industry still wrapped in a veil of mystery and misconceptions.

Nouriel Roubini
Professor of Economics at the Stern School
of Business, New York University, and
Chairman of Roubini Global Economics

Introduction

Anatomy
of a Hedge Fund

~

The Password Is . . .

> *Hedge funds are the ultimate in today's stock market—the*
> *logical extension of the current gun-slinging, go-go cult of*
> *success.*
>
> —Peter Landau, "Hedge Funds: Wall Street's
> New Way to Make Money" (*New York Magazine*, 1968)

FOR MUCH OF THEIR history, hedge funds have been viewed as exclusive, intentionally vague, high-risk investments that were only accessible to the *über*elite. Often referred to as "Wall Street's last bastions of secrecy, mystery, exclusivity, and privilege," they have generally been resented, misunderstood, and vilified for causing market turbulence and creating legions of wealthy people who seemingly have "more money than God." And yet, most do exactly what they say: They provide superior returns with less volatility. As such, investors continue to pour money into these alternative investments, with assets increasing from $38.9 billion in 1990 to $1.77 trillion in 2007 to $2.04 trillion in the third quarter of 2011.[1] With posted gains of 19.98 percent and 10.4 percent in 2009 and 2010, respectively, an increasing number of individuals and institutions are eager to gain insight and access into this secret society. However, many mysterious hedge fund managers often shy away from unveiling their profitable secrets.

Isn't it time that someone unravel the secret world of hedge funds? Isn't it time to provide intellectually curious people with a comprehensive overview of the industry without clouding it with jargon, negativity, and dry numbers? Isn't it time to help eager and cautious investors reap impressive gains while reducing overall market risk? Isn't it time to explain to the masses how hedge funds impact their pocketbooks even if they don't directly invest in this alternative investment vehicle?

Enter *The Little Book of Hedge Funds*. I'm your host. Anthony Scaramucci. Well, not actually your host—more like your trusted resident advisor. In 2005, I cofounded SkyBridge Capital Management, an alternative asset management firm that is now running approximately $5.7 billion in total assets under management by investing in over 35 different hedge fund managers. As an alternative asset manager and founder of the SkyBridge Alternatives (SALT) Conference, which is one the premiere conferences in the industry, I have been privy to cloaked conversations among some of the world's most successful hedge fund managers. I have listened carefully to their views on the industry, observed how they have ironed out market inefficiencies through their dynamic use of alternative investment strategies, and studied the ancillary literature written on the subject. And, as a managing partner of SkyBridge Capital, I witnessed my experienced staff thoroughly and thematically evaluate the quantitative and qualitative factors that go into allocating capital and selecting a hedge fund manager across all industry segments. And now, in this *Little Book of Hedge Funds*, I will pass this amassed knowledge onto you.

Consider this *Little Book* to be your personal guide to the hedge fund industry. We're going to provide you with a comprehensive overview of this secretive world, while exploring its impact on the overall market and global economy. We're going to explain the history and evolution of hedge funds and how they operate. Along the way, we're going to hear valuable insight from hedge fund luminaries and investing titans who have transformed the financial industry. And, we're going to do it all by using plain English—no jargon here.

After reading this *Little Book*, you will no longer have to shy away from conversations about *accredited* investors who allocate capital to hedge fund managers who take *two-and-twenty* by *exploiting market inefficiencies* through investment strategies (*short, hedge, leverage—oh my!*) that minimize *risk* while generating *absolute returns* . . . all in the quest for *alpha*. (Don't worry, you'll learn what all of this means in this book—just keep reading.)

Seeing the Forest from the Trees

Before we can delve into the money-making secrets of hedge funds, we must first define the term. And yet, in keeping with the mysterious nature of hedge funds, there doesn't seem to be a universally accepted definition. Perhaps the reason why many experts differ on the exact definition stems back to the origins. Although we will have a detailed history lesson in Chapter 2, hedge funds earned their name because they literally hedged. Once upon a time in a faraway land, a journalist named Alfred Winslow (better known as A.W.) Jones began managing his portfolio by selecting securities to be both long and short through leverage, thus, providing a hedge.

Although some managers still hedge, many hedge funds do not. So, what do they do? What do they all have in common?

As there is no magic formula for defining the term, but since this is the hedge fund industry, I want you to imagine that you are back in biology or anatomy class, peering over a pig—the capitalist kind. That's right. It's time to travel back to high school. Picture it. Freshman year. Biology lab. Pig dissection day.

You are sitting on some uncomfortable wooden stool, trying to look all macho and act all cool in front of your hot lab partner, who is deathly afraid of dissecting the small, fetal pig that lies before you. You strap on your boxy goggles, pick up the scalpel, and open up the pig (of course all the while smiling at your attractive lab partner). As you make careful incision after incision, you begin to extrapolate vital components of the pig's anatomy. With every piece you discover, you are learning the sum of the pig's parts, which will ultimately provide you with a better understanding of the overall makeup of the animal.

The same technique is needed to provide a definition of hedge funds. But instead of dissecting an animal, we are going to dissect the colloquial and controversial definitions presented over time by the experts.

Let's start with a technical definition provided by Jack Gain, president of the Managed Fund Association:

A pragmatic definition would be a private investment pool with a limited number of high-net-worth individual and institutional investors on the one hand and, on the other, a manager with the utmost flexibility.

Hmm . . . that definition doesn't say much, now does it? Besides, I've never been one for pragmatism. Let's keep moving.

According to the Alternative Investment Management Association's Roadmap to Hedge Funds:

> A hedge fund constitutes an investment program whereby the managers or partners seek absolute returns by exploiting investment opportunities (taking risk) while protecting principle from financial loss. The first hedge fund was indeed a hedged fund.

Sounds like a good definition to me . . . but let's take it further. Let's push the scalpel around a bit more. In *All About Hedge Funds*, Robert A. Jaeger defines a hedge fund as:

> An actively managed investment fund that seeks attractive absolute return. In pursuit of their absolute return objective, hedge funds use a wide variety of investment strategies and tools. Hedge funds are designed for a small number of large investors, and the manager of the fund receives a percentage of the profits earned by the fund.

Now we're getting somewhere, but this extrapolation is still missing something—firsthand knowledge from a legend in the industry. As such, we need to move our scalpel over the supercapitalist's heart so that we can see the following definition from legendary hedge fund manager Cliff Asness of AQR Capital. According to him, hedge funds are:

> Investment pools that are relatively unconstrained in what they do. They are relatively unregulated (for now), charge very high fees, will not necessarily give you your money back when you want it, and will generally not tell you what they do. They are supposed to make money all the time, and when they fail at this, their investors redeem and go to someone else who has recently been making money. Every three or four years, they deliver a one-in-a-hundred-year flood.

Although I may be biased toward my talented friend Cliff—who if he weren't running AQR might be writing comedy sketches for Jimmy Fallon or, better yet, could replace Seth Meyers on *Saturday Night Live*'s "Weekend Update"— his humorous definition is chock-full of vital information about hedge funds that completes the discovery process and enables us to fully learn the sum of a hedge fund's parts.

Now, although we may never agree on a universal definition of hedge fund, you will notice that all four of these definitions have a few terms in common. So, let's put down that scalpel and start examining the extrapolated components so that we can form our own definition.

- **Alternative Asset Classification**: Hedge funds live in the unique world of alternative assets, which— as the name implies—are investment vehicles other than the traditional investments of stocks, bonds, cash, or real estate. Alternative assets include other kinds of assets such as commodities, options, currencies, collectibles, convertible bonds, emerging market debt, and so on. Just as hedge funds lack a clear definition, so do their alternative asset parents. So when you hear the words alternative investments just think of anything in the investment world that is an alternative to stocks, bonds, and real estate and that utilize alternative trading strategies like hedging and shorting (don't worry . . . we'll get to those terms a bit later).

- **Absolute Returns**: As an alternative investment that uses alternatives to stocks and bonds, the returns that hedge funds seek are different. Unlike mutual funds that strive to outperform a relative index or benchmark such as the S&P 500 or Dow Jones, hedge funds utilize a bevy of alternative investment strategies in order to produce positive returns regardless of market conditions and fluctuations.[2] In other words, the goal of hedge funds is to deliver long-term growth of capital and achieve positive returns. Hedge funds produce these "absolute returns" by investing in alternative assets (referenced in previous section) with alternative investment strategies (referenced below).

- **Alternative Investment Strategies**: In order to produce these absolute returns that are disconnected from the stock and bond markets, hedge funds rely on a wide range of diverse alternative investment strategies that seek to mitigate risk while protecting capital and maximizing returns. Although we will discuss these strategies in detail in Chapter 7, they are classified into the following categories:
  - Long/Short Equity
  - Relative Value
  - Event Driven
  - Directional
- **Managers/Partners**: Just who are these magicians who employ these alternative investment strategies in the quest for absolute returns and how do they structure their funds? Primarily, hedge funds are

legally organized as limited partnerships, trusts, or limited liability companies (LLCs). Under this arrangement, there is one general partner who is equipped by the private placement memorandum to have discretion over the assets of the fund. The limited partners are the investors in the fund who are not fully liable—they are only liable for any losses that relate to their investment amounts. As such, many hedge fund managers "operate as general partners through another company as a way to avoid the unlimited personal liability, thus only exposing themselves to limited liability given the company serving as the general partner."[3]

Oftentimes, the general partner has his own money invested in the fund. In theory, this arrangement incentivizes and motivates the manager, while comforting the weary investor, because any investment decisions and/or results will impact the manager's personal pocketbook.

A word of caution—don't invest in a manager who doesn't have skin in the game and doesn't put his money alongside that of his clients or limited partners. There is nothing that concentrates the mind better than the fear of capital losses.

- **Fees:** How do these managers make money? Hedge fund managers typically charge two types of fees: a performance fee and a management fee. Infamously known as "two and twenty," the fees that a general partner typically makes are between 1.0 to 2.0 percent of the fund's assets under management *plus* 20 percent of the profits. Translation: if you put a million dollars into the fund, the annual management fee will be $15,000. The manager is then entitled to a percentage of the profits. So, let's say that the group has a gross return after the management fee of 20 percent. In this example, the manager gets $40,000 and the investor gets to keep $160,000. (We'll discuss this structure in more detail in Chapters 1 and 4.)

- **Accredited Investors**: Unlike mutual funds in which any Tom, Dick, or Harry can invest, hedge funds have historically only been available to "accredited" investors. In order to meet this criteria, individuals must have a minimum of $1 million net worth (excluding the value of the primary residence) and/or make more than $200,000 a year, while entities must have a minimum of $5 million in total assets (or entities the owners of which are all accredited investors).

- **SEC Regulation**: As of the writing of this book in January 2012, not all hedge funds are currently regulated by the U.S. Securities and Exchange

Commission (SEC), a financial industry oversight entity. However, it certainly seems that regulators are anxious to crack down on these alternative investment vehicles. As a result of this lack of regulation, hedge funds are able to invest in a wider range of traditional and untraditional securities using an array of investing techniques. Many funds in the industry—including SkyBridge—have embraced the regulation and are allowing regulators the opportunity to review their businesses for best practices.

Now let's bring the pieces all together to form a definition—a hedge fund is an alternative investment vehicle that seeks to produce absolute returns by utilizing a wide range of traditional and untraditional investment strategies that exploit market opportunities while protecting principal, preserving capital, and maximizing returns. These private investment pools are actively run by managers who typically invest their own money in the fund and receive a 20 percent performance fee, which consequently serves to align their interests with investors in the fund.[4] They are only available to accredited investors and are currently not all regulated by the SEC. (Boy! That was a mouthful!)

. . . what's that you say? You want to keep dissecting further? You want an in-depth overview of all of those components just referenced so that you can impress your friends at your next dinner party with your vast wealth of knowledge as it relates to this mysterious industry? You want a piece of the hedge fund universe? We'll get to all of that—and more—in the next 10 chapters.

Lifting the Veil

Have you ever tasted condensed milk? You get all of the creamy, rich, authentic, sugary taste of whole milk, without any of the fat, calories, or guilt. Consider *The Little Book of Hedge Funds* to be the same. It will be chock-full of synthesized information that will make you wiser and potentially more profitable, yet has none of the unnecessary, extraneous, high-brow content that will make you want to run for the hills. And, just as condensed milk is no substitute for the real thing, I'm not going to ask you to stop pouring whole milk in your cereal. I'm just going to expose you to an alternative. A hedge fund alternative.

Ready to take your first sip?

First, we'll explore the inner realms of the hedge fund world by defining and dissecting its core features and comparing this alternative asset to its more popular twin sibling—mutual funds. This crash course will be like an Italian Sunday dinner. We will load you up with information and fatten you up with a comprehensive knowledge base.

Then, we will move to a more technical space where we will learn about the various ways in which hedge funds actually make money. At this juncture, you will receive Jedi training on more complex subjects such as alpha, beta, and volatility. You will learn the various ways in which hedge fund managers exploit market anomalies and iron out inefficiencies through a series of "exotic" hedge fund strategies.

After that, I'll show you how you can invest in a hedge fund directly or through a more feasible alternative—a fund of hedge funds. My objective since starting SkyBridge Capital has been to open the window of access and transparency into the industry so that every dentist in America can have access to the world's finest money managers and feel comfortable when making their investment decisions. (You don't have to be a dentist, by the way . . . but you get the point.) In these middle chapters, I will show you how we do that in SkyBridge's day-to-day operations.

Finally, I'll suggest how you—or your son or daughter, nephew or niece, friend or foe—can get a job at a hedge fund so that you, too, can reap the benefits of a highly incentivized fee structure.

And, all along the way, you'll meet legendary, powerful, and wealthy hedge fund moguls who will candidly describe the hedge fund industry and its impact on global markets in their own words. In addition to reading their commentary throughout each chapter, you will also get inside the minds of the hedge fund gurus. At the end of each chapter, you'll read their responses to a series of four questions that allows them to talk about the industry in their own words.

So, are you ready to enter "Wall Street's last bastions of secrecy, mystery, exclusivity and privilege?"

Access granted. No password required.

Chapter One

What Is a Hedge Fund?

—❧—

The Traditional Long-Only Portfolio versus the Alternative Hedge Fund Portfolio

> *Hedge funds are generally perceived to be the investment of choice of the rich and the informed, and they are more interesting and fun to discuss than your Vanguard index fund.*
> —Cliff Asness, AQR Capital Management

THE YEAR WAS 1989. I had just started working at Goldman Sachs in the world of investment banking—the industry adored by many Ivy League students and business school graduates. A few floors up, legendary research director Lee Cooperman was asked by Goldman Sachs to create a mutual fund and lead the Asset Management Division. This long-only equity mutual fund was called GS Capital Growth.

Although Cooperman was extremely successful at picking stocks and examining company income statements and balance sheets, he was intrigued by the opportunity of starting a hedge fund, as he saw its potential to profit from smart stock picking even if the market seemed overvalued at times. And so, he approached the head honchos at Goldman, trying to convince them to start a fund. At the time, they passed as they were concerned over the consequences of shorting the stock of one of their investment clients. After all, no investment bank would want to put a sell recommendation in writing for fear of losing its relationship with the companies it covered . . . especially when there were advisory fees on the line. The thought of shorting a client company's stock back then was unthinkable. For Lee Cooperman, however, his passion was managing the money not managing the business.

Shortly thereafter, he started Omega Advisors. While his fund has experienced some ups and downs, he has had a spectacular career replete with great performance for his clients. The fund's ability to hedge risks through shorting, options, and derivatives has allowed his portfolio to have lower volatility and higher returns than he could have achieved in a classic mutual fund.

So, why am I telling you this story? Well, on a simplistic level, a *Little Book of Hedge Funds* just wouldn't be complete without a few big stories from big personalities who have become hedge fund legends. In fact, that is exactly what the hedge fund industry has become—big! Its managers' personalities. Its successes. Its failures. Its mystique. Its impact on the global market. Granted, it is a small, young industry that is still undergoing a maturation process, but this is an evergreen industry that has a big impact on the market and investors.

Right now we are witnessing an explosion in the hedge fund industry similar to the one the mutual fund business experienced more than 50 years ago. We are witnessing a transition of assets—and while there is competition from mutual funds, hedge funds will be a continued source of power in the world of money management.

So, back to my original question—why am I telling you all of this? In order for you to understand the hedge fund industry—its impact on the market and your investments— you need to first understand this alternative investing tool and how it differs from traditional asset classes such as mutual funds.

Although mutual funds are similar to hedge funds in that they are both pooled investment vehicles that invest in publicly traded securities in order to generate a positive return, there are a number of differences between these two fraternal twins. In this chapter, we will explore these differences. In doing so, we will gain a better understanding of the true meaning of a hedge fund so that you can better ascertain if it is an appropriate investment vehicle for your portfolio, while also helping you get a better sense of its impact on the overall market.

Comparing Apples to Oranges

Just ask any identical—or even fraternal—twin and they will tell you that their life has been full of constant comparisons and tradeoffs. Which twin is better looking? Smarter? More outgoing? More athletic? Better with numbers? Makes more money? Has the better education? You get the gist. Similarly, the financial world is riddled with unbalanced comparisons of financial products that render investors bewildered and uncertain. A frequent source of such comparison often involves mutual funds vs. hedge funds.

Mutual funds are the propeller plane, while hedge funds are the fighter jets. Mutual funds are the general practitioners in medicine, while hedge funds are the surgeons— generally the neuro kind. Mutual funds are the Breyer's Vanilla Bean, while hedge funds are Ben & Jerry's Cherry Garcia. Mutual funds are Guy Lombardo on New Year's Eve, while hedge funds are Mayor Mike Bloomberg dancing with (and kissing) Lady Gaga. Mutual funds are Rodney

Dangerfield, while hedge funds are Jon Stewart. Mutual funds are Berlin with the Wall, while hedge funds are Berlin with all the swank art galleries.

Have I satisfactorily crushed the mutual fund industry? I wasn't trying to. As your hedge fund muse, I was just trying to help you see that the mutual fund industry has matured and become prosaic, while the hedge fund industry has become cutting edge. But, let's base this comparison on facts not playful analogies. Let's start by comparing some definitions and performance, shall we?

According to the Securities and Exchange Commission, a mutual fund is a professionally managed investment company that invests clients' money in stocks, bonds, money market instruments, and cash. Although many brokerage houses would have an investor believe that this portfolio is composed of a wide set of subcategories including large-cap growth stocks, large-cap value stocks, municipal bonds, treasury bonds, and so on, most plain-old-vanilla portfolios are simply made up of stocks and bonds. And, as the old investment cliché goes, to figure out the exact allocation between these two birds, an investor should simply subtract his age from 100 to figure out what percentage he should allocate to stocks and then put the rest in bonds.

Now anyone who wasn't living under a rock during the fall of 2008 can certainly tell you how this long-only allocation can play out under adverse market conditions. While this blend of traditional assets may be a winning strategy during periods of steady and stable growth, it has been quite a disaster in the last decade. Consequently, it has caused many an investor to reevaluate his long-only cookie-cutter portfolio construction and rethink his portfolio mix.

That's where hedge funds—I mean the hedge fund comparison—come in. As we learned in the Introduction, a hedge fund is an alternative investment vehicle that seeks to produce absolute returns by utilizing a wide range of traditional and untraditional investment strategies that exploit market opportunities while protecting principal, preserving capital, and maximizing returns. These private investment pools are actively run by managers who typically invest their own money in the fund and receive a 20 percent performance fee. Although many hedge fund managers hold a diverse portfolio of stocks, bonds, and alternative investments, the typical allocation varies by manager and his investment strategy. In other words, hedge fund managers are less interested in a pie chart that divvies up a portfolio by offsetting slices; rather, they are interested in exploiting market anomalies and gaining an informational edge through a dizzying array of investment and trading strategies.

While I am not naïve enough to suggest that hedge funds performed well during the financial crisis, they did far less damage than a traditional stocks-and-bonds port-folio. In 2008, the hedge fund industry was down an average of 22 percent, which is much better than the market, which was down approximately 55 percent. Furthermore, according to Hedge Fund Research, an investor who put $1,000 in hedge funds at the beginning of 2001 would have $1,418.89 at the end of 2010 (inclusive of all fees and taxes). One who put $1,000 in the Standard & Poor's 500 in 2001 would have just $920.67 at the end of 2010.

As Ronald Reagan once said, "Facts are troubling things, they don't lie and are irrefutable." Hedge funds are products that, for the most part, have performed well in down or choppy markets. If you want to make money for yourself in the future and also find ways to potentially lose less money, then you need to spend the time to learn about the differences of hedge funds versus mutual funds.

Regulation . . . or Lack Thereof

According to the SEC report, "Hedging Your Bets: A Heads Up on Hedge Funds," the key difference between mutual funds and hedge funds relates to regulation—or lack thereof:

> Unlike mutual funds, hedge fund are not registered with the SEC. . . . In addition, many hedge

fund managers are not required to register with the SEC and therefore are not subject to regular SEC oversight. Because of this lack of regulatory oversight, hedge funds historically have been available to accredited investors and large institutions, and have limited investors through high investment minimums (e.g., $1 million).

Mutual funds are tightly regulated by the Investment Company Act of 1940, which requires them to invest in publicly traded securities according to their stated investment objectives. Some of the requirements imposed by regulators include releasing their holdings and performance to the general public, providing daily liquidity, valuing shares accurately and daily, and providing investors with a prospectus prior to investing.

Conversely, hedge funds are loosely regulated and currently do not have to register with the SEC or the Commodity Futures Trading Commission. And, let's face it, registration doesn't mean a hell of a lot these days considering that Bernard L. Madoff Investment Securities LLC was once registered with the SEC. (Allow me a quick soapbox moment: Although the media tag Madoff as a hedge fund guy, the irony was that he wasn't running a mutual fund or a hedge fund; he was running a separate account business that made tons of money and thousands of clients bucketed him in the world of alternatives. Regulation never stopped Madoff . . . the recession did.)

The regulations imposed upon hedge funds include the following:

- *Type of Investor*: As mentioned previously, hedge funds are only accessible to "accredited" individuals and institutions that meet specified criteria, which was updated in the summer of 2010. (We will discuss these criteria in Chapter 3.)
- *Number of Investors*: In addition, they are required to have no more than 500 limited partners invest in the fund.
- *Advertising*: No solicitation of clients through traditional forms of marketing and advertising. In taking a "fair and balanced" approach to any dissemination of information, a hedge fund must be certain to tread water carefully so as to get its message out while adhering to regulatory provisions.

At some point in the not-too-distant future regulators will find a way to more closely monitor the hedge fund space. In my opinion, this will not impair the ambidexterity of the industry or its respective investment process; rather, it will provide the necessary transparency and disclosures to protect investors.

Size: The Achilles' Heel

Hedge funds and mutual funds differ quite considerably in the amount of assets they manage. According to Daniel Stratchman, author of *Getting Started in Hedge Funds*, the largest hedge fund has more than $120 billion in assets under management, while the largest mutual fund complex has more than $2.7 trillion in assets under management. And yet, this is a quite misleading number as there are numerous hedge funds with less than $10 million in assets under management!

Hedge funds are not able to aggregate capital in the same way as some of the largest mutual funds. If anything, they will get bigger due to performance and organic growth, but they will never be able to remain true to total return objectives if they overscale as their growth depends on their ability to be nimble and dynamic.

What are the implications of this finding on the global market? As hedge funds are smaller than mutual funds and large banks, their investments have less of a direct impact on the overall move of the market. Moreover, as "small enough to fail" institutions, a hedge fund blowup generally does not require government intervention and taxpayer dollars, whereas "too big to fail" banks require such intervention.

That being said, the tremendous growth in the hedge fund industry—which has slowed down a bit since the

2007 to 2009 economic crisis—has often been described as the Achilles' heel for many funds and their bottom lines. Why? More funds equals an increasing amount of hedge fund dollars crowding similar trades and utilizing similar strategies, which equals diminished ability to execute trade and increase performance.

Think of it this way: Elephants don't fit in small bathtubs, but then again they don't get all of the extra pampering, either. Hedge fund managers need to be big enough to scale a disciplined and deep research and investment process but not so big that they deliver diluted returns.

Manager Fee: The Infamous Two-and-Twenty

Perhaps the most discussed difference between mutual funds and hedge funds is the fee and reward structure. Traditional investment funds—or those that generally invest in the stock and bond market—earn a fixed percentage of the assets they manage, passing along gains or losses to their investors. This investment management fee is equal to approximately 1 to 1.75 percent of assets under management.

Whereas mutual funds tend to only charge one fee that is based on assets under management, hedge funds demand two fees—an investment management fee of 1 to 2 percent of assets under management *plus* the performance fee of 20 percent of the profits earned. Often referred to as "two and twenty," a hedge fund manager's fee is directly correlated to his fund's performance. This linking of compensation to investment performance has both positive and negative effects on the industry—both in terms of its performance and perception.

On a positive note, performance-related incentive fees (as well as fixed fees) tend to attract more skilled, talented, and entrepreneurial professionals to the industry, which in turn, is said to be one of the main drivers of high returns. Makes sense to me. After all, it is not completely out of the realm to think that an incentivized fee structure with the opportunity for high rewards would attract top-level talent who have the self-confidence to make contrarian decisions. Just look at the New York Yankees!

On the other hand, critics argue that these asymmetrical and high fees harm investors in the long run. Once described as a "compensation scheme dressed up as an asset class," hedge funds do not usually require that managers give back a fee to the investor if the fund loses money. Conversely, mutual fund gains and losses must have a symmetrical effect, that is, the fee for the manager is the same regardless of the amount of over- or underperformance relative to a benchmark.

This incentivized fee structure has also caused quite a stir in the industry as critics claim it leads to excessive risk taking. And yet, the 2007 to 2009 economic crisis proved otherwise. As the reward structure of large banks is closely tied to the performance of the entire bank itself, critics of traditional investing claim that bankers may take unnecessary risk so as to achieve glamorous profits that will garner attention from upper-level management, which determines their bonuses. This compensation structure ultimately damages financial stability because it ties a shareholder's earnings to the performance of the entire bank.

In addition to the fee structure, hedge fund managers generally have their own capital in the fund, which theoretically aligns the manager's and investor's interests. According to Yale University endowment guru David Swensen, this arrangement puts greater emphasis on generating superior investment returns while protecting the risk of loss of principal. He says, "The idea that a fund manager believes strongly enough in the investment product to put a substantial personal stake in the fund suggests that the manager shares the investor's orientation."[1]

Although mutual funds and hedge funds are managed by professionals who make investment decisions on behalf of their clients, the fact that hedge fund managers often put their own money into their fund incentivizes them to protect their wealth as well as their income, which is riding on their performance. In having their skin in the game and in putting their money where their mouth is, they are further incentivized to ensure that their portfolios achieve positive returns.

As you can imagine, there are various pros and cons to this fee structure, which we will discuss further in Chapter 4.

Investment Strategies: The Long and the Short of It

As an alternative investment, hedge funds are able to operate in almost any type of market and use almost any type of investment strategy. Although the *New York Times* once referred to hedge funds' use of these instruments as "exotic and risky," it should be noted that most financial institutions use these "exotic" instruments . . . albeit in different capacities.

Short Selling

Generally, mutual fund managers are only able to hold "long" positions—in other words, they buy a security, such as a stock, bond, or any other money-market instrument, with the expectation that the asset will appreciate in value. They load up on "hot" stocks when the market is expected to go up and then sell these hot stocks when the market is expected to go down. Under this umbrella, investors usually shop a 60/40 portfolio—60 percent in stocks and 40 percent in bonds.

On the other hand, hedge fund managers are able to employ a diverse range of investing strategies that literally enable them to *hedge* their bets—hedging their investments to increase gains and offset losses. Similar to an insurance policy, these investment techniques are designed to prevent losses when another investment falls in price. (In 2008, however, what we learned is that despite past history most asset classes displayed high correlation. They all went down with few exceptions—cash and U.S. Treasuries.)

Although hedge fund managers also hold long positions in their portfolio, they are able to both **long** and **short** the market in order to generate positive performance and reduce risk.

Here's how this works: Managers split securities into two buckets—securities that they think will *rise* faster than the market and securities that they think will *fall* faster than the market. Then they take *long* positions in the first bucket (the risers) and *short* positions in the second bucket (the fallers). This enables hedge fund managers to neutralize market risk, take advantage of turbulent market conditions, and ensure that they'll make money whether the market goes up or down. Or, as hedge fund founder A.W. Jones says, "shorting enables you [to] buy more good stocks without taking as much risk as someone who merely bought."

Sounds simple . . . but it is quite the contrary. Playing the long/short game can be quite complicated. In order to short stocks or other securities managers need to be able to set up margin accounts. In other words, they must use **leverage**—that is, they must borrow money—to make more money and amplify the returns. Sound risky? It is . . . but we'll get to that in a minute. Right now, let's get back to the heart of the matter—shorting a stock. Here's how it works.

How to Short a Stock

Step 1: The hedge fund manager identifies a position that he thinks is overvalued in the marketplace—this finding is based upon a thorough analysis of the company's fundamentals and/or technical analysis. Alternatively, managers may get intel on the potential short position from their respective prime brokers.

Step 2: The manager borrows the stock from the prime broker and sells it into the market. (There used to be an uptick rule, meaning you could only short stock on a price uptick, but not any longer. Many people believe that this rule should be reinstated, but until it is, you can sell the stock right into the market.)

Step 3: If the manager is correct—as David Einhorn was about Lehman Brothers in 2008 and currently is with Green Mountain Roasters—that the fundamentals of the company are flawed and the stock is overvalued, there will be a steep drop in the value of the stock.

Step 4: The manager goes back into the market and buys back the stock at the lower price and returns the stock to the borrowing source.

Step 5: The manager pockets the profit, less the loan amount paid for the "borrow."

If the manager is incorrect and the stock rallies at some point, he will have to buy it back and he still pays the borrowing fee and loses money on the reversal. A massive buying panic is sometimes known as a "short squeeze." This occurs when there is positive news on a name that lots of hedgies are shorting; many of them will step into the market and buy the stock to effectively get out of the way.

How does this practice compare to the conventional mutual fund operating principles? Let's compare, shall we?

Imagine you are the Warren Buffett of stock picking— you are extremely gifted at selecting the best stocks and have a keen understanding of market conditions. And, as luck would have it, you were just given $100,000 to invest.

Let's say that you believe the price of GothamDay is overvalued at $100 a share (don't even bother looking up that fictitious stock—do you really think my compliance team would let me publish any actual stock advice?). In knowing that GothamDay has poor fundamentals you believe that the stock will fall. So, you borrow 100 shares of GothamDay from your prime broker and sell them for $10,000. A few months later, the price of the stock falls to $50. You buy the 100 shares back for $50 a share or $5,000, return them to your broker and pocket the difference—$5,000.

Sounds simple. Hardly. Shorting is hard. The fact is most managers don't do it well. It is a complicated mix of assessing fundamentals, understanding momentum and market psychology, being able to handle pressure, and having a sense of timing. It is almost like having to learn all of the fundamentals of investing by reading a textbook that you are holding up to a mirror—everything is backwards! Ever drive 65 miles an hour in reverse on a freeway? Didn't think so.

And, of course, this strategy only works if the manager is a skillful stock selector. What if your gamble didn't pay off? What if GothamDay produces a new product that rivals the iPhone and suddenly the stock rises to $250 a share? Ring ring—it's your broker calling and he wants his shares back . . . now! So, you have to buy the 100 shares you borrowed for $25,000, resulting in a $15,000 loss (plus broker fees). Ouch!

In sum, the ability to short gives hedge funds a sizable advantage over mutual funds as it enables a manager to potentially achieve higher returns while assuming less risk regardless of market conditions. In offsetting one's long positions through short positions (thinking = hedging), a manager decreases his net exposure to the market and consequently assumes less market risk. But, be careful, as shorting takes no prisoners.

Leverage

As you can see from the previous examples, a critical investing tool used among many hedge funds is leverage. According to the SEC, "many hedge funds seek to profit from all kinds of markets by pursuing leveraging and other speculative investment practices that may increase the risk of investment loss." Whereas a traditional mutual fund manager would only be able to invest with the endowment he receives, a hedge fund manager is able to use leverage to increase his endowment and increase or broaden his investments. Specifically, managers are able to borrow money from their prime brokers and use it to expand their portfolios so that their long positions and short positions are often augmented by borrowings. In other words, they are able to borrow money to make money (or lose money if they are wrong).

Again, let's say you were given $100,000 to invest. Here's how the scenario would work out with and without our good ole friend leverage:

- *Long-Only Investor*: As a traditional investor, you would put $60,000 in stocks and $40,000 in bonds. Cut-and-dried.
- *Short-Selling Investor*: In an effort to hedge your portfolio, you borrow $100,000 so that you increase your kitty to $200,000. This leverage enables the manager to buy $140,000 worth of good stocks while shorting $60,000 worth of bad stocks, thus giving him more money to play with so he can better diversify his portfolio. As a result, the hedge fund manager incurs less stock-selection risk and less market risk.

But, leverage can be a fickle bitch . . . just ask Long-Term Capital Management. As Warren Buffett says, "When you combine ignorance and leverage, you get some pretty interesting results." Leverage can be tricky as it bears various levels of risk—counter party risk and market risk. I compare this alternative investment tool to a very sharp knife coming out of the steering wheel of your sports car; it can point at your heart as you are traveling downhill on an icy mountain road. In other words, when you need leverage least, it can hurt you the most.

As a matter of policy, I disdain heavy leverage as it wipes out your ability to be anything less than certain. Any slight miscalculation or exogenous unpredictable market event can permanently impair the capital in your portfolio. It's sort of like the Wolf and the Three Little Pigs. No matter how brick house your conviction and analysis is, leverage can turn your portfolio into a straw house, and any slight wind can take that house down.

That being said, there are managers who know how to use leverage judiciously and with the right risk management and downside protection, the tool of leverage can be effective at enhancing returns.

Derivatives

Along the quest in the hedge fund crusade to mitigate risk and preserve capital, hedge funds also use fancy-pants derivatives, which are contracts between two or more parties where the price of the security is "derived" from one or more underlying assets. Derivatives make it possible to precisely target risk and reward. A stock option is an example of the classic derivative where one can enter into a contract with another based upon the price of a stock. A call option means that someone is betting that a stock is going up. A put option means someone is betting the stock is going down. Of course, their counter party is betting the opposite; this difference in opinion is what makes the market.

Some critics—including the Oracle of Omaha—have coined derivatives as weapons of mass destruction in the market . . . and for good reason. Back in 2008, AIG almost brought the world to its knees by not having enough capital on hand to make good on Lehman credit default swaps (CDSs), which are basically contracts that allow the buyer to buy insurance on a potential debt default. In other words, if I am worried that Lehman is going out of business I can buy CDSs on Lehman's debt. The contractor must then pay to make that debt whole in the event of a default. Guess what? AIG was selling this derivative but couldn't back it up in the event it ended up on the wrong side of the trade. AIG was like a bookie making a bet without having the dough on hand if the 60 to 1 long-shot came in and won. That would have been a financial market Armageddon had the government not stepped in and loaned AIG $85 billion to clear and make good on those contracts.

Liquidity: Swimming in Pools of Money

My grandfather used to say that "if you can't afford the price of the ticket, then don't go to the movies." The same can be said about liquidity, which is defined by Investopedia as the degree to which a security can be bought or sold in the market without affecting the security's price. This is where mutual funds have a significant advantage.

Mutual funds allow investors to place sell orders and remove funds on a daily basis. And when they say the check is in the mail . . . it literally is—within a week or less! They have a per-share price (called a net asset value) that is calculated each day, so you could sell your shares at any time. The reason for this high level of liquidity is attributed to the types of investments they hold. And, consequently, it defines the purpose of a mutual fund as a vehicle that generates asset inflows from investors rather than one that generates the highest level of performance possible.

As hedge funds seek to generate returns over a specific period of time they are typically not as liquid as mutual funds. (Ironically, hedge funds are able to engage in shorting because of their supply of liquidity or cash.) Critics of hedge funds argue that they use this slow-and-steady-wins-the-race mantra to justify "lockup periods" — which are periods of time during which investors cannot remove their money. They can be quarterly, biannual, or annual; they are rarely monthly and never daily. Although investors can withdraw their investments sooner, they can only do so at a price—a redemption fee.

Although certain hedge funds and funds of hedge funds—such as SkyBridge Capital—have developed products that have shorter lockup periods, many funds require long lockup periods. As such, people need to be careful about the percentage they allocate to hedge funds in their portfolio.

Over the course of my 25-plus-year career, one thing that I've learned is that a lot of people think they are long-term investors, until they have short-term losses. Know thy investing self. If you don't have a long-term investment plan, don't lock up your money.

So, Do They Actually Hedge?

Today the use of the word *hedge* when describing a hedge fund can be considered a misnomer. The reality is this: Many hedge funds do not hedge risk. If they did, there would be no return. Instead, hedge funds seek to hedge *certain* types of market risk while simultaneously exposing themselves to risk where they expect a reward from bearing the risk. As a result, their key priorities are to make consistent and stable returns over an established period of time.

The Proof Is in the Pudding

Mutual fund? Or hedge fund? What's an investor to do? Sure, he could just move to cash, but what's the satisfaction in that? It tastes sour; is less filling; and is less diverse.

Given the current state of the market, I recommend that all institutional, wealthy, and retail investors have hedge fund exposure. As evidenced by the preceding laundry list, the varying elements of hedge funds enable these investors to better diversify their portfolios so that over time they can better reduce risk, preserve capital, and reap healthy returns. Furthermore, the environment is ripe for an investment vehicle that has a well-rounded arsenal of tools, which pounce on market inefficiencies and give investors an edge in their portfolio construction. True, they may appear riskier than traditional vanilla mutual funds, but many of them are actually less risky and provide better returns.

That being said, hedge funds are not for everyone nor are they a substitute for other investment vehicles. For many people, mutual funds—with a swirl of alternative asset or hedge fund exposure—are probably the best option. It isn't a one-size-fits-all sort of approach; however, a portfolio of hedge fund portfolios can be sleeved into most investors' tactical asset allocation.

A word of warning: Before anyone invests in this industry, they must heed this surgeon general's warning—investing without proper due diligence or proper personal risk assessment can be bad for your mental and financial health. Do your homework. Be prepared. Have a proper screen. Research. Research. Research.

So, let's find out just who can invest in these enigmatic and stealth investment vehicles and how every dentist in the United States can get in the game.

In the Words of a
Hedge Fund Legend . . .

Leon G. Cooperman, Chairman, Omega Advisors Inc.

1. How would you define a hedge fund?

   A hedge fund is defined by a few distinct characteristics:

   a. Fee Structure where Managers Receive a Percentage of the Profits plus a Management Fee

   b. Long and Short Investing Strategy

   c. Multi-Asset Class Portfolio Construction

   d. Large co-investment by general partner leading to a complete alignment of interest

2. How or why did you get started in the industry?

   I worked at Goldman Sachs for approximately 25 years starting in 1967 and was elected to the partnership at the end of 1976. My principal roles at the firm were Partner in Charge of Research, Chairman of the Investment Policy Committee and in 1989 I started Goldman Sachs Asset Management. I retired from the firm at the end of 1991 to start Omega Advisors. At that time Goldman Sachs was reluctant to have a hedge fund as part of its product line and, since this was my passion, I decided to retire from the firm to pursue a new career path. To this day

I have maintained a great relationship with my colleagues at Goldman and have an extremely high regard for the firm. I am proud to say Omega Advisors is an investment option for their employees' retirement funds.

3. **What hedge fund strategies do you use?**

   At Omega we try to make money for our clients in five ways:

   a. Stocks are high risk financial assets and short-term bonds and cash are low risk, so we spend a good amount of time at the firm trying to figure out stock market direction, (e.g., are stocks undervalued going up or overvalued going down?). Let's face it, a rising tide lifts all the ships and a receding tide lowers them. Our view of the investment outlook importantly dictates our risk asset exposure.

   b. All the studies I have read regarding portfolio returns indicate that in any one year, more important than individual stock selection, is being in the right asset class. So we spend a great deal of time studying and assessing indicated and expected returns for stocks compared to bonds and in various classes of bonds, (e.g., high yield, investment grade and government). We do this globally. In essence, we are looking for the straw hat in the winter. People don't buy straw hats in the winter when they tend to be on sale.

c. Our most important activity is seeking and finding undervalued equities, mainly in developed countries.

d. Shorting overvalued stocks again in developed countries.

e. An occasional macro trade which would include currency, bonds, commodities and the major equity indices away from the S&P 500.

4. What do you see as the future of the industry?

The hedge fund industry is a cyclical growth business. I would guess that in 1968 the aggregate assets of hedge fund managers were less than $1 billion, with the largest fund being A.W. Jones & Co. with modestly over $200 million. Today, assets in the hedge fund industry exceed $1 trillion and these assets are managed by approximately 10,000 hedge funds with the largest being over $100 billion. If that isn't growth then I don't know growth.

I believe this growth will continue and that the incentive fee structure will continue to attract top-caliber talent. As long as hedge funds continue to generate superior returns, they will continue to attract superior talent, cash, and attention. After all, money goes where money is treated best.

Chapter Two

The Parlor Cars of the Gravy Train

~

The Long and the Short of It

Hedge funds were the parlor cars of the new gravy train. It was fitting that their key figure was a man who had taken up stock investing as a sideline, an elegant amateur of the market who liked to think of himself as an intellectual, above and beyond the profit motive.

—John Brooks, *The Go-Go Years*

THINK ABOUT IT: If it didn't exist somebody would have invented it. A system of money management that allows the manager and the capital to have an efficient, symbiotic, and symmetrical relationship. Here's the deal. There are boring ways to run money, the blunt instruments of asset management—long-only mutual funds and their arch nemeses, the exchange-traded fund (ETF) and the index fund. These products have their followers, and, of course, the true believers will assert the sanctity of their respective product lines with religious ferocity and certainty. Then there are the curmudgeons of finance, the Old Salts who have been there and done that. Can't fool them—ever—and while there is a sucker born every minute there are 10 sages born in a century, and each of them knows it all. There is no way to beat the market. There is no way to add value in the process. The laws of randomness can only fool you into thinking that you are making a contribution to the process. Yada, yada, yada.

And then came the hedge funds and the hedge fund guys and their stealth ability to iron out market inefficiencies by embracing four distinguishing features set forth by their founding father—Alfred Winslow (A.W.) Jones. And the hedge fund superheroes shortly followed: Barton Biggs, Julian Robertson, George Soros, Stan Druckenmiller, Michael Steinhardt, Cliff Asness, Steven A. Cohen, Jim Chanos, David Tepper, Dan Och, Leon Cooperman, Lee Ainslie, Dan Loeb, Ken Griffin, Paul Singer, the list goes on and on. Legends. Investing titans who have built hugely successful businesses and enviable track records.

Nah, the naysayers vilified these guys, contending that they were just "disguised beta" whose risky actions threatened global markets. Smug with certainty, the Old Salts—and a cabal of people who followed them—were convinced that the only order in the universe came from no one really ever adding any value in the money management process.

And yet, the history of hedge funds demonstrates quite the opposite. In seeking undervalued assets, managing risk, and speculating with their own money, these "super capitalists" have essentially sought to stabilize the market. In creating a club-like atmosphere of exclusivity, the industry has summoned a following of intellectually curious observers who have tried to access, replicate, or report upon their every move.

And so, the hedge fund movement—with its own progenitors, disciples, and followers—rages on. Paradoxically, its progression is contingent upon its history. So, let's examine the history of this industry. Sharpen your pencils. Take out your notebooks. It's time for a bit of a history lesson.

Inside the Olive Pit

Like any other history lesson, our story begins in ancient Greece with renowned philosopher Aristotle preaching to his disciplines about the mathematician, philosopher, and daydreamer Thales of Miletus.

Having predicted an abundant olive crop for the coming season, Thales struck up a deal with all of the local olive refiners in the region. In exchange for a large sum of money, he asked these unknowing farmers "for the right but not the obligation" to rent the entire olive pressing facility for a set fee for the duration of the year's harvest.[1]

As luck would have it, Thales' prediction proved to be true as the olive crop experienced a record-breaking harvest. But, alas, luck can take you only so far. Having strategically negotiated a deal with the farmer for the right to rent the olive press at a set fee, he was able to keep his costs steady and then turn around and charge a high premium for the use of the press—pocketing the difference.

And, so my observant readers, the first hedge fund-like practice was born—using contrarian investing practices and foresight to achieve high returns. Speculation, prognostication, and risk taking have been with us since the dawn of time. The hedge fund industry has taken it to a new level by refining the agreement between the speculators and their capital partners and by setting up a remuneration process that allows for heavy compensation for those who have bet correctly. Malcolm Gladwell, the best-selling author and pundit on all things related to the zeitgeist, believes the advent of big compensation—corporate and otherwise—came to fruition with Curt Flood. Flood, the St. Louis Cardinals outfielder who became the first free agent in the history of baseball, ushered in the dawn of unimaginable salaries for top-notch and in-demand talent. All-stars after Flood got paid, and paid like Croesus. As salaries began to grow to astronomic levels in sports, suddenly they were warranted in corporate America and the world of hedge fund investing.

The Secret Is in the Sauce

While the Thales tale is quite enjoyable to read (and was somewhat retold here for some humorous relief), it is generally agreed that the first hedge fund was created by A.W. Jones in 1949. After writing an article on financial forecasting trends for *Fortune* magazine, the former sociologist and journalist decided to launch the entity A.W. Jones & Co. with four friends. At the ripe age of 48, he and his pals invested $100,000 ($40,000 from Jones) in U.S. stocks by taking long and short positions that were augmented with a healthy amount of debt. Essentially, Jones and team believed that the long/short investment strategy would provide profits by hedging the risk of a market downtown and consequently yield positive returns regardless of the market conditions.

The magic potion for such euphoria: "Using a metric he called 'velocity'—a precursor to what is now called beta, the measure of how closely a stock's movement tracks the broader market—he split his holdings into two groups: good stocks that rose faster than the market in good times and fell slower than the market in bad times, and bad stocks that did the opposite. He took long positions in the former and short positions in the latter, theoretically ensuring that he'd make money whether the market went up or down."[2]

And voilà! In their first year, Jones and crew earned 17.3 percent and outperformed every mutual fund by 87 percent during the next decade. They had achieved irrefutable performance.

Who would have thought that the financial improvisation performed by a man who studied Marxist theory, drank with Dorothy Parker and Ernest Hemingway, and fought in a civil war would serve as a model for hedge funds. Oh, and did I mention that he didn't have an MBA or a PhD in financial engineering?[3]

Now, although I told you that there was not a universal definition of a hedge fund, each and every single hedge fund manager operates by Jones' basic tenets. So, take out those notebooks again, as it's time to summarize Jones' main contributions to the world of hedge funds.

Performance Fee

Not only did Jones develop the idea of an investment strategy designed to do well no matter what happened in the stock market, he also developed and implemented a closely tied payment and incentive structure. Just as the Phoenician sea captain kept a fifth of the profits from successful voyages, Jones and his managers earned a percentage—typically 20 percent—of profits. This notorious scheme remains typical for many of today's hedge fund managers. (And don't kid yourself—even investment legends like Benjamin Graham used this type of payment structure decades earlier. And while the most famous Graham protégé, Warren Buffett, is very critical of it, he has hired people into Berkshire Hathaway who were former hedge fund managers. We are all hypocrites—purists only exist in fiction.)

To this point, Jones was also influential in creating the structure of a hedge fund—a limited liability company (LLC). As an LLC, the managers were able to take a share of the profits earned on the investor's money. Moreover, managers were required to invest a portion of their own capital in the fund, thus aligning their interests with those of their investors. Although Jones and his team profited handsomely from this arrangement, the current profits oftentimes amount to billions and billions of dollars for the most successful managers. (Of course, using the word billions with such veracity will open up the industry to even more ridicule and scorn. Darn it, if they would only pay those rascal journalists a little more!)

Avoid Regulation

A.W. Jones was always a man of few words—lest we forget, prior to wearing his hedge fund manager hat, he ran secret missions for the Leninist Organization (an anti-Nazi group) and even married his first wife, socialist and anti-Nazi activist, Anna Block in secret! (Okay, okay—so the George Washington of hedge funds was a bit eccentric. Genius is closely aligned with the crazies.) And so it only followed that he would try to keep his hedge fund practices under the radar.

Although some folks believe his secrecy stemmed from his distrustful nature toward competitors as well as his appreciation for tax loopholes, his main reason for secrecy was to avoid regulation so that he could continue to sell short and remain a private entity. In an effort to avoid the limelight, Jones relied on word-of-mouth advertising and dinner party referrals and avoided advertising or the public solicitation of business.

As such, he is credited with having changed the entity from a general partnership to a limited partnership and having put on the hedge fund cloak of mystery.

Short Selling + Leverage

Perhaps most important, Jones' most profound influence on the hedge fund industry is his alternative and contrarian strategy of using short selling + leverage to achieve profits regardless of market conditions. Often referred to as the redheaded stepchild, short selling, which involves speculating on the prospect of corporate failure was seen as un-American in 1950. And yet, Jones embraced this "little known procedure that scares away users for no good reason" and viewed it as "speculative means for conservative ends."

Here's how it worked. While traditional investors loaded up 100 percent on stocks (think = Xerox or Polaroid) that were expected to rise (think = long-only), Jones decided to leverage (think = borrow) up to 150 percent. If the stocks appeared to be moving in the wrong direction (think = down), he reduced his exposure by selling short. In other words, he would leverage (again, think = borrow) those stocks from other investors and then sell them in the expectation that their price would fall. Once they lost their value, he would repurchase those stocks for profit. In doing so, he was able to insulate his portfolio from external market conditions and hedge out market risk. As a result of this method, his fund earned a cumulative return of 5,000 percent. Genius! Although some may say that these returns were just disguised beta (don't worry, we'll get to that term shortly), the history in all sectors of the economy has benefitted from his axiom.

Before we move on, I'd like to provide some commentary on people's perception of shorting. In many sectors, shorting is still considered un-American; however, I'd argue that it is quite the opposite. Our system prospers when it is based upon meritocracy and success borne from innovation and experimentation. The short seller keeps the rest of the crowd honest and corporate management teams on their toes. Oftentimes, he is the searchlight onto corporate fraud or bad corporate practices. While there is an argument to be made that short sellers can unfairly raid a company and force its demise through negative selling momentum (this has become worse with the elimination of the uptick rule where one could only short a stock on an uptick thus preventing or at least speed bumping negative momentum), this practice is essential for correcting market inefficiencies and for an economy that welcomes a free market system.

Okay, now that I got that off my chest . . . let's move on!

And the Beat Moves On . . .

In 1966, *Fortune* magazine journalist Carol Loomis coined the term "hedge fund" (somewhere along the way the "d" got dropped). And, suddenly it seemed that a host of Jones-like imitators were popping up everywhere . . . and 40-plus years later the trend continues.

According to various research reports, the U.S. Securities and Exchange Commission (SEC) claimed there were 140 hedge funds in existence by 1968. However, with the collapse of the "go-go-market," and the advent of stagflations and its bear market in the 1970s, many of these funds floundered—apparently, some overzealous managers neglected to hedge in their quest for big gains. "By one estimate, assets under management by the 28 largest hedge funds had declined by 70 percent by the end of 1970. Alas, the hedge fund phenomenon was viewed as fleeting."

And then came the 1980s and 1990s . . . and the emergence of celebrated hedge fund managers who favored global macro (think = big picture) hedge fund strategies. John H. Makin, a principal at Bruce Kovner's Caxton Associates, referred to this period by saying, "The extraordinarily high returns earned by hedge funds during their golden age in the 1980s and early 1990s were not too good to be true. They were just too good to be true for everyone."

During this time, many successful investors were lured into the hedge fund world and began operating under the scheme of raising capital and using unregistered funds to yield high returns. This, coupled with the growing interest in foreign investment, resulted in the rise of global macro funds, which accounted for 60 percent of the hedge fund industry in the 1990s, according to Oliver Schupp of the Credit Suisse/Tremont Hedge Fund Index.

Perhaps the most famous trade in global macro history occurred in 1992 when George Soros' and Stanley Druckenmiller's Quantum Fund famously "broke the Bank of England." In realizing that the Bank of England did not have sufficient reserves to defend the British pound against devaluation, they began selling massive quantities of sterling quicker than a liquidating jewelry shop. Consequently, the British government was forced to withdraw the pound from the European Exchange Rate Mechanism, netting his fund over $1 billion. Talk about a transfer of wealth! Britain's taxpayer dollars literally fell into Soros' and Druckenmiller's pockets. For much of the 1990s, Quantum managed returns in the 30 percent range.

Perhaps equally as influential was Julian Robertson and his Tiger Fund. Robertson successfully negotiated the purchase of the Russian government's entire stock of nongold metals in 1998. Considered to have most closely followed Jones' hedge fund methodology, he, at one time, had in excess of $20 billion in assets under management. According to Robert Burch, Jones' son-in-law, "Julian is the natural successor to Jones. He has built a business around the principles and disciplines that Jones used to build his business. He understands the Jones model and uses it to make superior returns regardless of market conditions."[4]

However, his greatest impact on the industry may indeed lie in the generation of hedge fund managers that his genius spurred. Known throughout hedge fund land as "Tiger Cubs," nearly 20 percent of all assets run by money managers were once employed by Tiger.

Other large players emerged from the hidden cloak of mystery, including Paul Tudor Jones' Tudor Investment Corporation, James Simons' Renaissance Technology, and Louis Bacon's Moore Capital. And there were hosts of others, including Tom Steyer, Richard Perry, and Oscar Shafer, all of whom had a competitive edge that they were exploiting in the markets to yield absolute returns and great performance.

The Revenge of the Nerds

In early 2000, hedge funds were in trouble. Despite the success of a few managers who successfully navigated the tech stock world, many hedge funds fell victim to the speculatory market that was saturated with growth stocks. As investment vehicles that sought to exploit market efficiencies, the philosophy and strategies traditionally implored by hedge fund managers did not jive with market trends . . . and trends they would later prove to be.

According to one legendary manager, "No traditional Graham and Dodd investor [value investor] invested in AOL. They shorted it. And they got fucked."[5] The same was true for legendary managers like Julian Robertson, whose Tiger Fund fund had been overtaken by "mouse clicks and momentum" and George Soros, whose Quantum Fund fund was down 21 percent.

But just as it seemed that these last bastions of wealth were about to fade into the distance, a new character joined the cast of wealthy investors who was winning to invest hoards and hoards of capital needed to refuel the fire: endowments.

Led by Yale University's David Swensen, the marriage between hedge funds and endowments ushered in a new outlook for hedge funds (although I'd love to go on and on about this partnership, I will do so in the next chapter. So for now, let's just say . . .). No longer thought of as simply an alternative investment vehicle for the 1 percent, institutional investors were able to commit floods of capital—much more than an individual can provide. Swensen, one of his generation's leading chief investment officers, changed the rules and deemed it safe to wade deeper into the hedge fund investment pool.

Since then, a rising number of institutional investors— such as public pension funds, endowments, private pension funds, and foundations—have been allocating larger portions of their portfolios to hedge funds so as to improve returns while reducing systematic risk. While hedge funds were once considered an elite investment tool for wealthy individuals, approximately 61 percent of hedge fund assets are now owned by institutions. Furthermore, the largest endowments (those with over $1 billion in assets) were said to invest approximately 23 percent of their funds in hedge funds in 2010. Consequently, a flood of money has poured into these funds, increasing the impact hedge funds have on the market and global economy, and affecting the everyman's pocketbook.

And Now for the Not-Quite-as-Successful

By the mid-90s, it appeared that hedge funds had found the Shangri-La of investments. But just as they were about to meet the leprechaun and his pot of gold at the end of the rainbow, it happened—Long-Term Capital Management (LTCM) collapsed in 1998 and was later rescued by the federal government.

Founded in 1994 by a proprietary trading legend, John Meriwether from Solomon Brothers; two Nobel Prize-winning economists, Robert C. Merton and Myron Scholes; and a slew of finance wizards, LTCM used an arbitrage strategy that exploited temporary changes in market behavior. By pair trading and betting on price convergence over a range of scenarios (we'll discuss those strategies in Chapter 7), the LTCM band of brothers leveraged their $4 billion fund until it had a notional exposure of over $1 trillion dollars. Fear not, with propellers spinning on top of their heads, they were sure that they were making the right investment decisions based on the historical models.

Having achieved astronomical levels of success and financial leverage, they began taking riskier bets and used derivatives to take "unhedged" positions in the market. In other words, they began betting with money they didn't have in the hopes that the market would revert back to normal. In 1998, they placed an enormous bet—we're talking about leveraging up 70-to-1—on the turbulent Russian financial market.

Yet something unexplained happened along the way to the forum. In August of 1998, the Russian government decided that it could not meet its debt obligations and started to devalue the Russian ruble. As Russian bond prices cratered, traders around the world began to scramble and sold the bonds and other securities to create liquidity and to meet margin calls. Despite the mathematical purity of their assumptions and their analysis, the überconfident LTCMers were caught off guard. They were in an untenable position. When the Russian government defaulted in 1998, LTCM blew up, losing millions and millions of dollars a day. As Warren Buffett says, "You only find out who is swimming naked when the tide goes out."

Fearful that LTCM's collapse would signal a more widespread hedge fund fire, the Federal Reserve board intervened and orchestrated a $3.65-billion bailout—with the help of 14 other financial institutions. Each of the major broker dealers (with the exception of Bear Stearns) put up capital, took over the defunct fund, and worked patiently to unravel the trades once the market calmed down. According to the Fed's William McDonough, "An abrupt and disorderly liquidation would have posed unacceptable risks to the American economy." Sound familiar?

Although Long Term Capital Management took the crown for the most-documented hedge fund failure, the runner-up is more than likely Amaranth Advisors. Founded in 2000, Amaranth Advisors successfully bet on the natural gas market and came up big, showering its clients with sparkling performance. And then came the summer of 2006. Thinking that there might be another Hurricane Katrina-like event that would result in the explosion of natural gas prices, Amaranth bet the farm and put all of its eggs in the natural gas basket. As we all know, no significant natural disaster occurred in 2006 (thank goodness). And so, with over $9 billion in assets under management, a 32-year-old, Ferrari-driving trader lost a $6 billion bet on natural gas futures in 2006. But, this time around, the fireman sent in to extinguish the fire was another hedge fund named Citadel.

■ ■ ■

The media does a great job of focusing our attention on these sorts of spectacular wins or thunderous losses. Little ink is wasted on investments that pick-up small profits on mundane price discrepancies. Yet, that is where most of the hedge fund industry's bread is made and buttered.

Emerging from the Ashes

The hedge fund failures referenced previously were nothing compared with the financial crisis that the world experienced (and is arguably still experiencing) from 2007 to 2009. Although all investment vehicles have been vilified by the press, investment banks, housing lenders, money market funds, and insurers experienced the largest losses. In 2007, hedge funds ended the year up 10 percent. By the end of the debacle of 2008, they were down 21 percent while the S&P 500 Index was down almost twice as much to 37 percent (see Table 2.1).

Table 2.1   Comparable Performance: HFRI Fund of Funds vs. S&P 500 TR

	2007	2008	2009
HFRI Fund of Funds Index	10.25%	−21.37%	11.47%
HFRX Global Hedge Fund Index	4.24%	−23.25%	13.40%
S&P 500 TR	5.49%	−36.99%	26.47%

Source: Data provided by PerTrac, Hedge Fund Research, Inc.

One hedge fund manager, John Paulson, was even able to profit from this mess. Sensing that the economic cycle was about to experience a downturn, he began targeting mortgage securities in 2005. With a $2 million budget, he brought in Paolo Pellegrini, who bought the largest mortgage database in the country and hired a team of analysts to study it to figure out the past patterns of default rates. Although they proved to be unsuccessful in 2006, the tides began to turn in 2007—by February 2007 the fund was up 66 percent, and by the summer of 2007, he literally made a billion dollars in one day.[6] His gamble had paid off. As you can imagine, the response to Paulson's genius was not well received.

All of this said, hedge funds did suffer tremendously from 2007 to 2009. With heavy losses occurring in the credit market, many hedge funds were losing money at an alarming rate. The culprit behind their demise: leverage. Some funds got caught in overleveraged positions (Think = Sowood Capital), while other funds desperately needed access to leverage but were unable to borrow money because of the fear and panic imposed by the collapse of too-big-to-fail Lehman Brothers. To add insult to injury, the government stepped in and imposed restrictions on short selling—taking the bread and butter tool from an industry whose very livelihood depended on it. By the end of 2008, approximately 1,500 hedge funds were forced to sell their portfolios or shut down, while others lost tremendous amounts of capital and some legendary managers even lost their stellar reputations. And yet, despite the wreckage, hedge funds weathered the storm . . . mystique intact.

Where Are We Now?

In 2010, the International Monetary Fund estimated world investments at 22.9 percent of the gross world product, which equates to roughly $14.5 trillion. Using the Hedge Fund Research calculation of $1.9 trillion in hedge funds at the end of 2010, that means that 13.1 percent of all of the world's investments are in hedge funds. That is a staggering number! And this number is expected to rise, with estimates claiming that the industry will triple and run over $6 billion within the next decade.

As you are reading this *Little Book*, there is probably some smart, young, overambitious contrarian investor starting a hedge fund. This unknown person is developing and deploying an investment thesis and strategy that will take advantage of market inefficiencies, minimize risk, and yield excess returns. Over time, his successes—and then his failures—will become the media's guilty pleasure. And when they do, there will be countless stories written about his investing genius, skillful prowess, big and contrarian trades, overabundant and luxurious real estate, one-of-a-like art collections, and board memberships. Against this backdrop, the industry will continue to grow; the best and the brightest from top-tier Ivy League business schools will continue to flock to an industry that was started by a mysterious journalist who developed a legendary investing (and payment) scheme; high-net-worth investors will continue to pour money into these private pools in the hopes of achieving alpha-like returns that will fulfill their champagne wishes and caviar dreams; and mainstream Americans will continue to be fascinated by a cloaked industry whose mystique paradoxically lures the attention it was intended to avert. And through it all, hedge funds will remain the alternative investment that not only makes money, but perhaps more important, rationalizes the irrational market by flattening out the kinks in the global market.

In the Words of a
Hedge Fund Legend . . .

Barton M. Biggs, Managing Partner, Traxis Partners

1. How would you define a hedge fund?

   A hedge fund is a pool of money run by a small number of cocky, arrogant souls who charge outrageous fees including a carried interest and expect to shoot the lights out.

2. How or why did you get started in the industry?

   I began running a fund for Alfred Jones and the first hedge fund A.W. Jones & Co. back in 1964 when I was an analyst at E.F. Hutton & Co.

3. What hedge fund strategies do you use?

   I am a macro hedge fund manager and am inclined to concentrate on financial assets which I consider to be my circle of competence, in other words I don't dabble in commodities and currencies.

4. What do you see as the future of the industry?

   I think the hedge fund industry is entering an environment where fees will be under extreme pressure. However it will still be the most lucrative destination for talented and lucky investors, and I believe it will continue to grow but at a slower pace than in the last decade.

Chapter Three

Accessing the Inaccessible

~

From the Elite to Main Street

Hedge fund investors are no longer an elite core of the world's wealthiest investors. Publicity about sustained superior returns attracted hoards of money into funds.

—Michael H. Steinhardt, legendary hedge fund manager

POP QUIZ: HOW ARE human beings attracted to something?

Answer: Tell them they can't have it.

As Groucho Marx once said, "I don't want to belong to any club that will accept me as a member." After all, the word *exclusive* comes from the word *exclude*. Imagine that—you're told you can't have something and then what? You immediately think to yourself, "I gotta have it."

Think about it—when the government banned liquor in the age of Prohibition, speakeasies popped up serving rogue alcohol. The result: people flooded in the doors. The same happened in the world of finance. When the government said only "sophisticated investors"—a code phrase for rich enough to burn money—can invest in hedge funds, access points popped up.

Historically, hedge funds were only accessible to the very wealthy and superelite. As private funds they were able to avoid most of the disclosure requirements of U.S. securities laws. In exchange for this lack of regulatory oversight, money managers could not solicit the general public through any form of "communication published in any newspaper, magazine or similar media." Historically, they had to rely on word-of-mouth, dinner-party-marketing to score wealthy clients who were primarily their business associates, family members, and friends.

With high minimums and access restrictions, these private bastions of wealth maintained an exclusive aura similar to that of an inaccessible speakeasy that only admitted the choicest of clients. At the time of their origin, only 3,000 investors accessed the 150 unique investment partnerships, which operated "almost completely out of public view."[1] With the average investment equaling $300,000, many of the investors bore such recognizable names as Laurence Tisch, Jimmy Stewart, and Lana Turner. Thus, a typical hedge fund database appeared more like a Who's Who List than a client roster.

As such, hedge funds became playgrounds for the rich folk who liked to walk around their respective country clubs, sniffing to their friends, "Not only am I rich, but I'm also smart enough to invest in a hedge fund." With the effect of nostalgia, this era was deemed a golden one—a time where managers and investors waltzed. Not a time of disco music and rap.

Although it is a bit more difficult today to discover just who exactly invests in hedge funds, solicitation is still frowned upon, access is still determined by wealth, and only 500 people are able to invest in a single fund. With funds requiring $500,000 to $10,000,000 to get in the door, exclusivity still rules the roost. And yet, over the years, the tides have begun to turn. With the advent in 1998 of 3(c)7 funds, access opened and became unlimited, provided that higher minimum net worth standards were declared. No longer investment vehicles for only elite and wealthy individuals, hedge funds are now primarily accessed by institutional investors.

It's All in the Name

Given the seemingly complex nature of hedge funds out-
lined in Chapter 1, regulators have imposed accessibility
restrictions on the types of people who can access hedge
funds. Interestingly enough, the recent changes in regulation—as well as the proliferation of financial information
and technology in the marketplace—have led to an increase
in hedge fund investors. "By not allowing fund managers
to advertise or market their businesses, the SEC has created a veil of secrecy over the industry that really helps the
managers attract business," says an industry insider.[2] Just
like the forbidden fruit, people naturally want what others
can't have. Hedge funds are no different.

Unlike mutual funds that are open to the general public, hedge funds are only accessible to accredited individuals and institutions that meet the specific criteria as set
forth in the Dodd-Frank Act, which is commonly referred
to as the Financial Reform Act that was signed in 2010.

- **Individuals**: In order to invest in a hedge fund,
  individuals must have a minimum net worth of $1
  million (excluding the value of the primary resi-
  dence) and/or make more than $200,000 a year.
- **Institutions**: Entities must have a minimum of $5
  million in total assets (or entities the owners of which
  are all accredited investors).

More specifically, Rule 501 of Regulation D defines an accredited investor as:

1. A bank, insurance company, registered investment company, business development company, or small business investment company.
2. An employee benefit plan, within the meaning of the Employee Retirement Income Security Act, if a bank, insurance company, or registered investment adviser makes the investment decisions, or if the plan has total assets in excess of $5 million.
3. A charitable organization, corporation, or partnership with assets exceeding $5 million.
4. A director, executive officer, or general partner of the company selling the securities.
5. A business in which all the equity owners are accredited investors.
6. A natural person who has individual net worth, or joint net worth with the person's spouse, that exceeds $1 million at the time of the purchase, excluding the value of the primary residence of such person.
7. A natural person with income exceeding $200,000 in each of the two most recent years or joint income with a spouse exceeding $300,000 for those years and a reasonable expectation of the same income level in the current year.

8. A trust with assets in excess of $5 million, not formed to acquire the securities offered, whose purchases a sophisticated person makes.[3]

Apparently earning a minimum annual income + having a net worth of more than $1 million = significant and sophisticated investment knowledge. Who knew?

■ ■ ■

Fools and their money are quickly parted, and we have watched very rich people act in very unsophisticated ways. Maybe years from now regulators will require an IQ test or a note from a psychiatrist or possibly a rectal exam (Lord knows many of us have our brains down there!), but until then read the partnership documents carefully and seek out professional advice before investing. Both sophisticated investors and unsophisticated ones have a need for protection against risk. With careful analysis and the right due diligence and asset allocation one can achieve this goal by using hedge funds as an investment tool.

The Institutional Invasion

In early 2000, hedge funds were in trouble. Julian Robertson's Tiger Fund had been overtaken by "mouse clicks and momentum." George Soros' Quantum Fund was down 21 percent and Stan Druckenmiller was leaving the fund after a dozen years; they, too, would be closing the curtain on their original proposition. "Markets have become extremely unstable," Soros said at an April 28, 2000, press conference. "We have come to realize that a large hedge fund like Quantum Fund is no longer the best way to manage money."[4] Just like that, the world's two largest and most profiled hedge funds had ceased to exist. The state of the industry was in question.

But just as the mystical world of hedge funds was down on its luck, a magical fairy godmother arrived in the form of a "still-backed Midwesterner" from Yale University who would change the shape (and portfolio) of hedge funds for years to come.

A Reluctant Buyer

In 1985, David Swensen, the former Salomon Brothers swaps legend and James Tobin protégé, took an 80 percent pay cut from Lehman Brothers to take over Yale's University's endowment. At the time, Yale's stale portfolio was in dire need of resuscitation, boasting a meager 10 percent allocation to alternative assets. Having studied under Tobin, he knew that the portfolio lacked diversification.

In an effort to better diversify Yale's stocks and bonds portfolio and reduce the endowment's overall risk, Swensen was cautiously intrigued by the prospect (and associated profits) of investing with hedge funds. And yet, he had little desire to do business with any hedge fund manager who simply sought fortune and fame by charging high performance fees. And so, it took the Wall Street transplant over five years to invest with the persistent Tom Steyer of San Francisco–based Farallon Capital Management. (Tom, of course, is now a legendary hedge fund investor who got his start on the Goldman Sachs risk arbitrage desk.)

Clearly ahead of his time, Swensen invested $300 million in Farallon in January 1990. Suddenly, institutions of academic excellence—such as Yale and Harvard—were given the reins to actually invest their endowments and development-earned dollars with hedge funds. As with all practices in higher education, other institutions jumped on the hedge fund bandwagon. From 1990 to 2000, the typical university endowment investment grew from 0 percent in hedge funds to 7 percent. And, in the years that followed, these universities were well rewarded, with gains of approximately 10 percent. Yale, in particular, was successful, generating $7.8 billion of the $14 billion in its endowment from hedge fund investments by 2005. (In 1999, David Swensen wrote a groundbreaking book entitled *Pioneering Portfolio Management*, where he shared his insights and careful analysis with fellow investors.)

And so, higher education administrators, who now saw hedge funds as a legitimized and credible cash cow, saved the day. As a result, hedge funds began to see a shift in audience—no longer were they only used by high-net-worth, wealthy individuals; institutions wanted a piece of the action, too. And who can blame them? While the market fell approximately 40 percent after the dot-com collapse, the average hedge fund did not lose money. Still sore from these self-inflicted wounds, institutional investors were happy to pay the notoriously high "two-and-twenty" hedge fund fee for downside protection against market turbulence.[5]

A Piece of the Pie

Since then, a rising number of institutional investors—such as public pension funds, endowments, private pension funds, and foundations—have been allocating larger portions of their portfolios to hedge funds so as to improve returns while reducing systematic risk.

Once considered an elite investment tool for wealthy individuals, approximately 61 percent of hedge fund assets are now owned by institutions rather than private investors. This is a 36 percent increase from 2008 when the figure stood at 44 percent.[6] Consequently, floods of money have poured into these funds, increasing the impact hedge funds have on the market and global economy.

As investors continue to pour money into hedge funds, assets under management have increased from $38.9 billion in 1990 to $1.77 trillion in 2007 to $2.04 trillion in the third quarter of 2011.[7] Who, in particular, is responsible for this growth? Refer to Figure 3.1 for a breakdown of investment types in hedge funds.

As you can see, approximately 60 percent of hedge fund assets are held by public pensions, endowments, private pensions, and foundations. Moreover, from 2007 to 2010, public pension funds have increased their investment allocation to hedge funds from 4 percent of assets under management to 7 percent.

Figure 3.1　Hedge Fund Breakdown by Investment Type

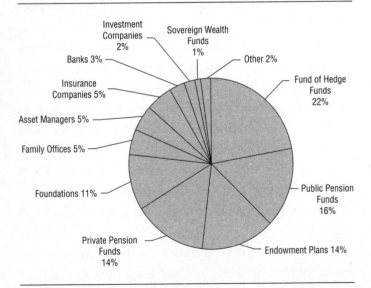

Source: Prequin Research Report, 2010.

A quick note—the largest portion belongs to funds of hedge funds, which, as the name implies, are funds that invest in other hedge funds. As these investment vehicles hold approximately 30 percent of institutional investments in their portfolio, it is safe to say that institutions own closer to three-quarters of all institutionally owned hedge fund assets.[8] (In Chapter 9, we will discuss funds of hedge funds in further detail and how you can utilize this investment vehicle to access this secret society.)

Take Out Your Measuring Stick

We interrupt this discussion on access for an important news bulletin. . . .

Size doesn't matter? Sure. And men read *Playboy* for the articles. In the hedge fund industry, size certainly does matter. And, in this industry, the motion in the hedge fund ocean has fewer waves for the biggest ships.

It would be impossible to state the exact number of hedge funds. In early 2007, there were said to be more than 9,000 hedge funds, 351 of which managed $1 billion or more.[9] However, as a result of the 2007 to 2009 economic crisis, approximately 5,000 hedge funds failed.

That said, the global hedge fund industry has experienced almost a 50-fold increase in the last 20 years.[10] This growth is primarily attributed to the compounding returns that derive from reinvested returns earned by the funds themselves. In other words, assets under management growth is a direct result of asset appreciation and income generated by fund investments. Specifically, 40 percent of growth has come from new capital given to funds by their clients, while 60 percent of growth has come from reinvested returns. Therefore, the key is to grow business from within instead of relying on new clients.

A word of caution: be careful when reading about the size of a fund. Critics question whether the size of the industry hinders a manager's ability to exploit market inefficiencies. The age-old question remains: Can the elephant move around in a small bathtub? Or, are small hedge funds unable to make big moves? The debate lives on. As such, it is important for investors to understand their total return goals first and then worry about the fund's size. It isn't a cop out to have a little of both.

We will now resume our regularly scheduled program. . . .

What It Boils Down To . . .

My objective since starting SkyBridge Capital has been to open the window of access and transparency into the industry so individuals can be comfortable when making their investing decisions. Our goal is to make sure that investors of all types can have access to the world's finest money managers—not just the $50 billion investor but the $50,000 one, as well.

That being said, for many people, hedge funds are not a substitute for mutual funds or other investment vehicles that enable them to invest in an index at a relatively low price. As I indicated in the previous chapters, many investors should simply add a slight percentage of hedge fund exposure to their portfolio. The mutual funds and exchange-traded funds (ETFs) just aren't sexy enough, and there is something about the bright stars in the hedge fund industry that attracts the highbrow elite investors.

Taking another perspective, hedge funds are necessary investment tools for institutions, high-net-worth investors, and retail investors who are seeking a vehicle that will diversify their investments, better manage risk, and deliver reliable returns. Just ask Yale and Harvard, whose endowments respectively returned 11.8 percent and 8.9 percent annually between 1999 and 2009—yes, even during the financial crisis!

Moreover, analysis suggests "that a modest allocation to hedge funds would improve the returns to public pension funds by approximately $13.67 billion annually." We live in an era of underfunded pension liabilities. Can you feel the groundswell of continued reallocation into the industry? In addition, an allocation of 10 percent of assets to hedge funds would yield an additional $1.73 billion in expected returns per year to endowments.[11]

So, while many peoples' pocketbooks may not directly benefit from hedge funds, the institutions that serve these same many people do. As a result of these extraordinary returns, these institutions are better able to serve the needs of their delegates. Moreover, these returns provide institutions with predictability. Whether granting scholarships or offering health care, institutional investors all have the same thing in mind: more money, less volatility. (Hey, who knows? Maybe it will rival the old Miller Lite slogan: Tastes great, less filling.)

In the Words of a Hedge Fund Legend . . .

Andrew K. Boszhardt, Jr., Managing Partner, Great Oaks Venture Capital

1. How would you define a hedge fund?

   A hedge fund to me at its most basic form is a private investment partnership whose objective is to make money for its investors while limiting long-term capital risk. It should always balance the twin objectives of maximizing return while limiting risk to protect permanent capital. Though there are an almost infinite number of investment strategies that could be applicable to hedge funds, indeed as many as there are possible investments and investable assets in the world, our strategy is one that is value-centric. That is we try to buy either distressed assets at a large discount to our estimates of recoverable value on one end, to buying growth stocks in world-class companies when they are reasonably priced. And of course there is an infinite number of situations in between these strategies that could be applied to our investment portfolio to add value.

2. **How or why did you get started in the industry?**

My partner and friend at Goldman Sachs, Anthony Scaramucci, and I were restless at Goldman and decided in 1996 to leave Goldman to start a hedge fund, Oscar Capital. We felt that our combined talents could synthesize to succeed in the hedge fund world. We had a blast building the business through highly volatile markets and successfully sold our firm to Neuberger Berman in 2001. Needless to say, we learned a great deal in these first five years on our own.

3. **What hedge fund strategies do you use?**

We are value centric, whether investing in distressed "flea market assets" or buying out-of-favor growth stocks at reasonable, or better yet, cheap prices.

4. **What do you see as the future of the industry?**

The hedge fund business has a bright future as it combines both the best investors in the world, with sophisticated investors looking for both higher returns and alternative/low risk-adjusted investment strategies.

Chapter Four

Heads We Win; Tails You Lose

Eating Your Own Cooking while Enduring Symmetrical Glories and Punishments

Ever since the 1960s, the 20 percent performance fee has excited envy and alarm—surely this heads-I-win-tails-you-lose format promotes wild punts with clients' capital . . . these complaints about hedge fund incentives seem plausible—until you take a look at the alternative.
— Sebastian Mallaby, *More Money Than God*

ON A COLD, DARK day in New York City, legend has it that Senator Chuck Schumer called 20 or so successful hedge fund gurus to meet with him at an Italian restaurant on the Upper East Side. The date was January 2007. Guests included Jim Chanos of Kynikos Associates, Rich Chilton of Chilton Investment Company, Steve Cohen of SAC Capital Advisors, Stanley Druckenmiller, Paul Tudor Jones II of Tudor Capital, and David Tepper of Appaloosa Management.[1] Although the media waited with bated breath to receive leaks from any one of the notable legends gathered around the table, the only press that hit the newswire dealt with the combined assets under management of those men attending—which was estimated to be close to $200 billion! What was talked about none of us will ever know, but the size and magnitude of the wealth and assets under management, by itself, became a news sensation.

Where does all this wealth and money come from? According to hedge fund folklore the true essence of a hedge fund is defined by the way in which managers get paid. The typical hedge fund charges the notorious two-and-twenty, which is an annual management fee of 2 percent of assets under management *plus* a performance fee that is equal to 20 percent of the current year's returns. In other words, a hedge fund manager who has $1 billion in assets under management is guaranteed $20 million a year in fees alone—and that's before he takes his 20 percent of any returns!

Spouted about by both Main Street and Wall Street folks alike, this payment structure perhaps has been the largest source of discontent toward the industry—even more heated than the discourse surrounding the hedge fund industry's involvement in the financial crisis of 2008. Even legendary investor, and recent tax activist, Warren Buffett, has criticized the typical compensation structure calling it a "grotesque arrangement"; others have characterized it as a "compensation scheme dressed up as an asset class." Ouch!

Yet, hedge fund managers rationalize this scheme claiming that it incentivizes their performances, while covering their overhead—hey, everyone should be entitled to the basic luxuries that office supplies, like pens and pencils, right?

Keeping Up with the Joneses

As mentioned previously, the hedge fund fee structure originated with A.W. Jones. Although he did not charge a management fee, he demanded a 20 percent share of the investment profits; no other payment was required.

As the number of hedge funds tripled in the 1990s, so did their management fees. Legendary managers like Michael Steinhardt and George Soros were suddenly imposing a management fee of 1 percent *plus* the 20 percent profit share. Since then the structure has grown further, with some managers charging a management fee as high as 4 percent. (When I entered the hedge fund industry, someone asked me at a conference where I thought fees were going over the next 15 years. "Down," I said with a degree of absolute certainty. Wrong. Wrong. (And wrong again. . . .)

Further still, other managers charge various fees based on the strategy or style the investor chooses. For example, hedge fund guru Stevie Cohen charges as much as 50 percent of the profits without a management fee, while other times he charges the standard fee of 1 percent plus 20 percent of returns.

Here's how the typical hedge fund fee structure plays—actually I should say pays—out. Let's say an investor invests $1 million in We Rock Asset Management. Operating under a 1.5 percent management fee *plus* a 20 percent performance fee, the We Rock manager will take 1.5 percent of $1 million dollars—which is equivalent to a fee of $15,000, which is payable over the course of a year in quarterly installments ($3,750 per quarter). As this fee is taken from the $1 million, the manager needs to make back the 1.5 percent before he can have a shot at making the performance fee. Let's assume that the manager is having a good year and produces a gross return of 20 percent; he will make 4 percent of the 20, and the client will net 16 percent. In this scenario, the manager will pocket $15,000 in management fees *plus* a $40,000 performance fee for a grand total of $55,000 per client (the client will have made $160,000). On the other hand, if the manager loses money, he will have to get the investor back to even before the performance fee kicks in. This is known as a "high-water mark," which we will discuss at length next.

A Bit of Protection

In an effort to add a bit of protection for investors and ensure that a manager is only paid if he generates positive returns, some hedge fund managers have a high-water mark and, in some cases, hurdle rates.

A high-water mark is basically a checks-and-balances system for investors that ensures a manager does not collect a penny of his performance fee unless the fund is over its previous high level. Essentially, it renders the performance fee eligible only on new profits rather than on profits that are recovering from previous losses.

A hurdle rate refers to a certain level above which the manager charges a performance fee. In other words, a manager is only able to receive a performance fee if the fund's performance is above a set benchmark rate.

Critics argue that these high-water marks and hurdle rates may cause disgruntled and fickle hedge fund managers to engage in some risky and reckless investing practices. For instance, let's say it's December 15 and the fund hasn't made any money. The critics argue that the fund manager may be motivated to be reckless and bet on esoteric securities in an effort to gamble his way to profits. While there is no doubt that some of this has happened in the industry, it is an overblown criticism. Most managers wouldn't want to take on that sort of business risk.

The Ends Justify the Means

Have you ever watched *Diners, Drive-Ins and Dives* on the Food Network? You know, the show where celebrity chef and sunglasses-sporting Guy Fieri drives around the country in a red '57 Chevy tasting the hidden gems at local eateries? Recently, I asked him what he says to a chef who prepares him food that is unappetizing and tasteless. The John Holmes of food porn's (never have I seen a person have more food orgasms on TV) response: "I say, this is *interesting*." Why am I recounting this humorous and honest story in a *Little Book on Hedge Funds*? Because the same response can be applied to the way in which hedge fund managers justify their fee structure—it's interesting.

Perhaps the most *interesting* way in which hedge funds justify their fee structure is by putting their money where their mouth is; having their skin in the game; eating their own cooking? Okay, okay. Don't throw your *Little Book* at the door. I'll stop with the expressions, but the truth of the matter is that hedge fund managers generally have their own capital in the fund, which theoretically aligns the manager's and investor's interests. As a general partner in the fund, the hedge fund manager is oftentimes the single largest investor in the fund and is discouraged from making external investments. By having their skin in the game, they make money right along with their investors; consequently providing incentive to have their fund yield high returns. This arrangement puts greater emphasis on generating superior investment returns while protecting the risk of loss of principal, because it incentivizes the manager to protect his own wealth and income. On the flip side, this *interesting* arrangement also gives some investors more confidence as their money manager will experience symmetrical punishments if their investment bets go wrong. A classic heads-*we*-win-tails-you-lose-*we*-lose example.

On a more simplistic level, hedge funds justify their fees by saying they pay for their overhead. After all, you can't expect a hedge fund manager to work without an oversized office on Park Avenue or in Greenwich, Connecticut—where would he put his computer or Ego Wall! Furthermore, these fees pay the bills—from lawyers to accountants to third-party vendors, to external vendors. All of these *interesting* justifications are captured in the fund's offering documents. As they can often get buried, investors must be sure to thoroughly examine these documents and read the fine print.

Moreover, managers claim that this structure gives partners the incentive to be opportunistic and take calculated risks that lead to superior performance and generate positive absolute returns. Typically, a managing partner is also an investor in the fund. By having their skin in the game, they make money right along with their investors, and consequently have incentive to make their fund yield high returns.

Lastly, they also justify this fee structure by claiming it attracts the best and brightest to the hedge fund industry, which, in turn, helps them yield high returns for their investors. Although this justification may sound a bit wishy-washy, it's not entirely unreasonable to think that an attractive incentive plan will lure the people with the most investment knowledge and accomplished pedigrees. It's the same reason that every high school basketball player wants to play with Kobe and the Lakers—they are actually an NBA team that makes money, pays their players, and wins championships.

Don't believe all of this *interesting* justification? Put yourself in the shoes of a recent college graduate who just moved to the Big Apple in the hopes of scoring a killer job so he can afford a killer apartment and land a killer girlfriend. A mutual fund manager offers him a job with a base pay and a small bonus that is tied to his performance. On the other hand, a hedge fund manager offers him a job with a base pay and a percentage of the profits. Which should he choose? This *Little Book of Hedge Funds* has shown us that in an equal asset world with equal performance, the hedge fund managers are going to make more money. This explains the brain drain from traditional money management firms and a brain flight into the world of hedge funds.

Want to know something that is even more *interesting*? This incentive fee structure will yield more money for the fund's clients. The proof is in the numbers: Let's say that you invested $100 in Steinhardt's fund in 1967. At the time of the fund's closing in 1995, you would have made $46,224, while that same $100 would have only earned you $1,706 if you had invested in the S&P 500. And that was after the fund lost significant sums in 1994![2]

Even Cowboys Have the Blues

But let's be honest here—not every hedge fund earns these vast amounts of money for its investors. For every hedge fund that yields these excessive returns, there are hedge funds managers just chugging along with the market and milking investors along the way as they gather their fixed performance fee just for showing up—and in some cases not even showing up!

As I mentioned at the beginning of the chapter, many critics—even legends like Warren Buffett—have been vocal in their disdain for these payment arrangement. In one of his famous Berkshire Hathaway annual reports, the Oracle of Omaha revisits the fictitious world of the Gotrocks family—a single family whose wealth he claims is being eroded because of the investment expenses they incur on their quest to yield high returns by working with various financial advisors and brokers. In applying this concept to the two-and-twenty crowd, he argues:

> In 2006, promises and fees hit new highs. A flood of money went from institutional investors to the two-and-twenty crowd. For those innocent of this arrangement, let me explain: it's a lopsided system whereby 2 percent of your principal is paid each year to the manager even if he accomplishes nothing—or, for that matter, loses you a bundle—and, additionally, 20 percent of your profit is paid to him if he succeeds, even if his success is due simply to a rising tide.

> . . . The inexorable math of this grotesque arrangement is certain to make the Gotrocks family poorer over time than it would have been had it never heard of these hyper-helpers. Even so, the two-and-twenty action spreads. Its effects bring to mind the old adage: When someone with experience proposes a deal to someone with money, too

often the fellow with money ends up with the experience, and the fellow with experience ends up with the money.

Mr. Buffett's assertion has merit—after all, there have been some less-than-honest hedge funds that are nothing more than a mutual fund or a "compensation scheme dressed up as an asset class." But, the reality is that the entire industry gets a bad rap simply because of the poor performance or business practices of a few funds.

Moreover, lest we all forget that other investment vehicles—including mutual funds—charge a management fee, as well. Although it is often lower—say 1 percent—and is not accompanied by a performance fee, studies have shown that mutual funds do not beat the market. As such, investors are paying for beta, not alpha, which translates into lower returns for infinite costs.

But, believe what you want—after all, the criticism is plausible. The bottom line is that money managers—both hedge fund managers and traditional money managers—come in all shapes and sizes. Some make money for their clients; some lose money for their clients.

That being said, investors have a choice in this free market. That's right—the trump card in this whole scheme is the free market and free choice. A hedge fund manager cannot put a gun to the head of an investor who is choosing to pay the fee. End of story. As such, investors must ask themselves what type of investment vehicle is the most appropriate given their investment goals. Based upon that answer, they must then ascertain which money manager possesses the best-equipped toolbox and skill set to help them achieve these objectives and make money.

By the way, my friends, back in 1956 Mr. Buffett himself had a hedge fund and operated more than 12 hedge fund partnerships until 1970. Furthermore, is it any more grotesque a fee arrangement than to fly on NetJets, a Berkshire Hathaway subsidiary? Please pass the carrots with the hypocrisy; I need my night vision.

As the expression goes, "Let he who is without sin, cast the first stone." And let hedge fund managers who are incentivized to perform, make the next big trade.

In the Words of a Hedge Fund Legend . . .

Steve Tananbaum: Chief Executive Officer & Chief Investment Officer, GoldenTree Asset Management

1. How would you define a hedge fund?

Maximum flexibility to go long and short company capital structures and financial instruments to generate absolute return. The manager is compensated with a management fee and an annual performance fee.

2. **How or why did you get started in the industry?**

I was a long-only manager at Mackay Shields and was recruited to work at a hedge fund. I enjoyed where I was working and suggested that I run an account for that hedge fund at Mackay Shields. Fortunately, the hedge fund owner agreed and that was my first experience running a long short fund.

3. **What hedge fund strategies do you use?**

Opportunistic credit.

4. **What do you see as the future of the industry?**

I believe we have already seen significantly more institutionalization in the 12 years we have been in business. Clients will demand more standardization in regards to investment process, security pricing and reporting and the overall control environment. I also believe that liquidity will better match strategies in order to maximize returns.

Chapter Five

The Alpha Game

⸿

In Search of El Dorado

Gaily bedight,
A gallant knight,
In sunshine and in shadow,
Had journeyed long,
Singing a song,
In search of El Dorado.

But he grew old—
This knight so bold—
And o'er his heart a shadow
Fell as he found
No spot of ground
That looked like El Dorado.

—Edgar Allan Poe, "El Dorado"

IN 1849, EDGAR ALLAN POE masterfully wrote the allegorical poem entitled "El Dorado," whose two-of-four stanzas are stated at the beginning of this chapter. According to the legend, El Dorado was thought to be a magical, unattainable city of gold that led many a brave men to their untimely and tireless demise. And yet, many a noble knight continued to search for this mystical world that was impossible to find in the physical realm.

Although hedge funds didn't exist during Poe's time, his never-ending quest for a land of wealth and spiritual treasures seemingly mirrors that of a hedge fund manager—to achieve alpha, the land of absolute returns. Often referred to as the Holy Grail for investors, alpha is attained when a manager achieves positive, nonvolatile returns no matter the movement of the market. These returns are entirely reliant on the investment skill of the hedge fund manager and are uncorrelated to the market index.

Just as many skeptics would have you believe that El Dorado is a fictitious place that can never be found, so do many academics prophesize that the investment world is a zero-sum game where alpha—excessive returns regardless of market conditions—does not exist. Naysayers argue that there are few money management geniuses who possess the intrinsic skills to achieve uncorrelated returns. Like our gallant knight, many hedge fund managers have similarly met colossal disappointment, glorious failure, and financial ruin—both for themselves and their clients—in their quest to achieve alpha.

I'm not going to mince words here; in the real world, alpha is a little easier to find than the unreachable El Dorado, but not by much. Many will strive for it. Few will succeed. And those who are actually able to find it, often negate its benefits by charging performance fees that gobble it up. And, yet, this chapter does not begin on such a morose and helpless note. What we propose is that alpha is rare but not entirely unattainable. It is not the manifestation of a series of coin flips on the road to a random market walk. Hedge fund managers are adding value through pure investment skill, and there is a system in place to discern those contrarian money managers who are actually able to find El Dorado.

On the pages that follow, we will discuss this alpha and beta game as well as the shadows that we meet along the way on this journey: volatility, correlation, and diversification.

But before we do, a quick word of caution. Some of the material that follows may be a bit confusing. If you are an undergraduate or graduate student, my guess is that you may be learning about these concepts for the first time. Don't worry—the glazing of your eyes is a natural process in the quest for knowledge. In the late 1980s when I picked up the classic books *How to Buy Stocks* and

The Money Game, I only had a partial clue as to what was going on. Concepts like margin and credit spreads as well as net present value were foreign to me. But, the only way I learned these esoteric terms was by diving in headfirst. Sure, there were times when I wanted to rip my hair out of my head, but soon enough I was dreaming in math equations and standard deviations. . . . and soon you will be, too. And trust me, when you are cashing in your big paycheck, you'll agree the pain was worthwhile.

The Alpha-Beta Song

Hedge funds have been further differentiated from other types of investments because of their exclusive quest for alpha. Alpha is the measure of a fund's average performance independent of the market. Thought to reflect a hedge fund manager's investment acumen, these returns are uncorrelated to a relative benchmark and have low volatility. For example, if a fund had an alpha of 2, and the market returned 0 percent, then the fund would return 2 percent for the month.

Of course, one cannot talk about alpha without talking about its much more attainable red-headed stepsister, beta. Beta is the measure of a fund's volatility—the level of systematic risk—in comparison to the overall market, which is generally measured at 1. Generally correlated against the S&P 500, a beta that is *greater* than 1 indicates that the fund is *more* volatile than the market, while a beta that is *less* than 1 indicates the fund is *less* volatile than the market. For example, if a fund had a beta of 2, and the market returned 1 percent, then the fund would rise to 2 percent.

If a fund has a negative beta it means it is moving in a completely opposite direction to the market. While this does happen temporarily and usually with great price shocks, negative beta is usually reserved for hedging instruments like puts or futures.

In case you are still taking notes, allow me to simplify the terms:

- **Alpha**: Money that a hedge fund makes through active stock picking or other types of security picking. These returns are *uncorrelated* to the market.
- **Beta**: Money that a hedge fund makes or loses through its exposure to the market. These returns are *correlated* to the market.
- **Volatility**: The statistical measure of risk or uncertainty as it relates to change in a security's value.

Uncorrelated! Correlated! I know what you are thinking—come on, Scaramucci, stop throwing these fancy vocabulary words at me. Sorry, guys. . . . not only am I going to keep the terms coming, but I'm about to throw in another history lesson here. Don't get too angry. At least you'll have some solid vocabulary in your arsenal to throw down at your next dinner party or job interview.

Another Theory, Another Definition

Just three short years after A.W. Jones began using a metric he called velocity to measure how closely a stock's movement tracks the broader market, a young graduate student named Harry Markowitz was busy at work developing the Modern Portfolio Theory. Discussed in a paper entitled "Portfolio Selection," this theory postulated that it was not enough to simply maximize returns but one must maximize *risk-adjusted* returns, whereby returns would be based upon a given level of inherent risk. The key to his theory was that the risk of a portfolio is dependent upon the relationship among its securities. In other words, if you picked the right securities or had the right asset allocation you could get out on the efficient frontier and actually find a scenario where you earned more reward yet took less risk.

Back in the 1950s, the problem with this approach was that it was not easy to implement—there simply wasn't enough time or resources to calculate the correlations between thousands of stocks—or (at that time) just 25! And so, picking up where Markowitz left off, William Sharpe put a spin on this theory and simplified it by calculating a *single* correlation between each stock and the market index (rather than calculating multiple relationships). And then James Tobin came along and put the icing on the modern portfolio cake; he urged investors to make one decision about what stocks to buy with their actual savings and then make another decision on what stocks to buy based on how much risk they wanted to take. And, voila— the one near-free lunch in economics was born: modern portfolio diversification. It was an academic recipe to make money in markets without losing the farm.

But, hold up a second—I'm getting ahead of myself, mentioning some fun financial lingo like "free lunch" before talking about how to select assets that enable you to control your portfolio's volatility and reduce risk. Let's step back for a second, shall we?

What is a correlation? And how do we find sources of uncorrelated returns? According to the fine folks at Investopedia, correlation is defined as a statistical measure of how two securities move in relation to each other. This relationship is quantified by a range between −1 and +1. If two securities have a +1, they will move in perfect unison and in the same direction—like two peas in a pod. If two securities have a correlation of −1, one will move up while the other moves down, and they will move in the opposite direction. If two securities have a correlation of 0, they will move completely independent of one another.

To further illustrate this point, let's says that you had two positions that were perfectly correlated to one another—let's call them the Jets and Patriots. If you invested $1 million in the Jets and $1 million in the Patriots and the two moved together in lockstep, your total risk exposure would be $2 million. Now, let's say that you had two positions that were uncorrelated to one another. If you invested $1 million in the Jets and $1 million in the Bulls, your total risk exposure would come to $1 million multiplied by the square root of the number of positions, which would equal x.

At this point, it can get a bit more complicated as you add positions; however, historical volatility and correlation can give you a better sense of how the overall portfolio will perform in different market and economic scenarios. And, the more you introduce a new uncorrelated position to the portfolio, the more risk can be reduced.

Driving with One Foot on the Brake

In their quest for alpha, hedge fund managers scour the playing field searching for sources of uncorrelated returns. Why? Uncorrelated returns = controlled risk. Think of it like a seesaw. As one side moves up, the other side moves down, thus balancing both sides. Similarly, uncorrelated returns balance the average risk a portfolio would have if each investment was considered independent of one

THE ALPHA GAME   [89]

another. As one position moves up while the other position moves down, the risk cancels out . . . well, at least most of the time (but we'll get to that a bit later in this chapter). What you don't want to have happen is that they cancel each other out and provide no return. Through analysis and thorough research, hedge fund managers hope for movements that actually create alpha—that is, they will move in a way not necessarily predicted by the overall market and will generate a healthy-sized stable return.

How does this all happen, you ask? Through the magical power known throughout the land as diversification—a risk management strategy whereby investors put uncorrelated positions in their portfolio so as to yield higher returns and reduce risk. Loosely translated: Don't put all your eggs in one basket.

In knowing the fundamental relationship between risk and reward, diversification involves more than simply holding a traditional portfolio full of stocks. As discussed in Chapter 1, financial advisors would have investors believe that the easiest way to provide an increased level of diversification is to load your portfolio with stocks *and* long-term government bonds as they generally have a low correlation with each other. However, the 2007–2009 economic crisis proved that being long in securities of different asset classes and/or being in cash isn't enough protection.

Intuitively, the best bet is to create a portfolio that blends various positions that represent various levels of risk and reward, while remaining aware of the extent to which the expected returns are correlated to one another. In other words, alternative assets—such as real estate, private equity, commodities, and foreign equities—should be added to the portfolio so as to theoretically increase returns and reduce volatility by diversifying risk. If done skillfully and thematically, this type of portfolio should generate alpha.

Putting Theory into Practice

Enough theory—let's get on to some practice here. How should an investor properly determine the level of risk to take? Simple—He must look at the stocks he actually owns *plus* the varying relationships (think = correlations) among them. After this analysis, the investor is better able to construct a portfolio that optimizes his expected levels of returns based upon a given level of market risk. In doing so, the hedge fund manager's goal is to mix up the portfolio recipe so that the reward is still there while taking less risk.

For example (a very simplistic example), let's say you have a portfolio of simply U.S. stocks and foreign stocks. As these two positions are highly correlated to one another, you do not have diversification, and, consequently, you have not mitigated risk. On the other hand, let's say that you have a portfolio composed of U.S. stocks and oil. As these two positions are generally uncorrelated and move independently of one another, you have diversified your portfolio and consequently mitigated some of the associated risk. (At the time of this writing, U.S. stocks and oil have had a long history of reverse correlation. If the tides have turned by the time you are reading this *Little Book* and for some reason they have become two peas in a pod, look elsewhere for your source of diversification and uncorrelated positions. That's a core lesson in this *Little Book*—always expect the unexpected and adapt.)

On a much higher level, let's say that you notice two similar items that are priced differently in different markets. In an effort to exploit the price differences of the identical positions, you take long and short positions, as they seem to have a perceived level of pricing convergence. In practice, a manager can buy the debt of a company and short its stock or use a portion of the income derived from the coupon to buy puts.

When deployed appropriately, the portfolio is actually able to generate positive returns even though price movements could actually go in an unintended direction. Thus, the goal of the alpha-seeking manager is to always manage the downside while making sure money can get made with a touch of diversification, reduced volatility, and risk.

A Word of Caution

In the 1980s, Long-Term Capital Management (along with its legendary credit arbitrageur leader, John Meriwether) was one of the first hedge funds to quantify the estimate of the correlations among various trades and mathematically measure risk through a technique known as "value at risk." Although we learned of LTCM's eventual demise caused by hubris in Chapter 2, Meriwether, Robert Merton, and Myron Scholes helped facilitate the correlation model.

Which brings me to an important note on correlations—as Warren Buffett famously said after the 2007–2009 crash, "Beware of geeks bearing formulas." While correlation is a helpful tool in the market, security and portfolio analysis should never be overly reliant on formulas. Formulas are like records; they are made to be broken or, in this case, disproven. These tools and techniques can enhance your ability to construct an alpha-generating portfolio, but they must be used with a heavy dose of common sense.

Sometimes Diversification Just Ain't Enough

Like the popular Patti Smith monster ballad "Sometimes Love Just Ain't Enough"—well, popular for just about anyone who listens to light FM, has gotten stuck in an

elevator, or who has been through a horrific breakup—
sometimes diversification doesn't pay the bills. In fact, sometimes it leaves you footing the check. In a 1998 letter to
investors, legendary fund manager Julian Robertson of
Tiger Management explained why this seemingly magical
tool wasn't able to save his fund from losing 10 percent of
his $20 billion-plus fund. "Sometimes we are going to
have a very bad month," he wrote. "We are going to lose
money in Russia and in our U.S. longs, and the diversification elsewhere is not going to make up for that, at least
not right away. You should be prepared for this."

Of course, this wasn't the first or the last time diversification would be left standing alone to reap the blame.
The financial crisis of 2007 to 2009 put a lot of academic
theory and proven financial application into question.
Chief among the defendants: diversification. To the sur-
prise of many investors, seemingly uncorrelated positions
all did the same thing—they all went down; clearly, there
was a leak in the canoe. It seems that in periods of panic
where liquidity is drained from the market, the historical
measures do not hold. This is why I have an honest skep-
ticism about overly quantitative approaches to investing.

Let's face it, despite what most risk strategists say,
the 10,000-year flood happens every five years on Wall
Street. What can go wrong, will go wrong. This is why
I sometimes use the phrase di-WORSE-ification to imply

that ill-conceived diversification can have a negative effect on a portfolio. The trick is to not overdiversify, then you look like everyone else or perform in line with the market. The skill here is to get enough diversity to mitigate some risk without diluting the positive impact that your investment themes can have. It is an art—a manager must have conviction, themes, and even some concentration; all the while making sure that he has some stuff going on that protects his downside in case he is wrong. There is nothing more devastating to capital or a portfolio than certitude without a tinge of uncertainty.

And, lastly, diversification has been criticized because it may be too expensive for investors to adequately diversify their portfolios. As a result, many investors forgo hedge funds and work directly with mutual funds as they can prove to be an inexpensive source of diversification. While I will never be able to convince everybody that the best players in the hedge fund industry deserve the fees, the hard facts prove the net performance of many hedge funds are superior to that of mutual funds. The net performance numbers—even including a fee for a fund of hedge funds—are providing investors with a sizable return with less overall risk. It isn't exactly El Dorado, but it is a place where money can go to grow and be preserved.

The Bottom Line

Mark Twain once wrote that you should "put all your eggs in one basket and watch the basket." Although this is an effective strategy for accumulating wealth, it is not effective for the hedge fund manager who is searching for the land of uncorrelated returns in his quest for alpha and riches. Diversity is required for the best managers who seek to protect and enhance wealth by taking calculated risks that yield excess reward. As such, the generation of alpha is the Holy Grail for investors.

In the Words of a Hedge Fund Legend . . .

Steve Kuhn, Partner, Pine River Capital Management

1. How would you define a hedge fund?

   An investment vehicle that seeks to leverage the collective experience and talents of its personnel to create absolute returns on the basis of skill, as opposed to market beta.

2. How or why did you get started in the industry?

   Shortly after graduating from college, I was introduced to the U.S. mortgage market. I loved the challenge of incorporating both quantitative skill and qualitative understanding regarding public policy and borrower prepayment behavior. I find this as fascinating today as I did when I began in the 1990s.

3. What hedge fund strategies do you use?

My team and I consider ourselves relative value traders, primarily seeking opportunities in mortgage-backed securities and other related market sectors. We seek to create value both by identifying specific trading opportunities and by dynamically shifting capital to those opportunities that look most attractive.

4. What do you see as the future of the industry?

The landscape for mortgage-backed hedge funds has changed dramatically since the financial crisis of 2008. Key capital providers including Fannie Mae, Freddie Mac and Wall Street trading desks have either exited the market or are dramatically reducing their involvement. We think this will increase the size and breadth of the opportunities in the mortgage market for many years to come. We also believe that hedge fund investors will continue to commit capital to mortgage strategies to seek out uncorrelated return streams, improve portfolio diversification, and achieve high risk- adjusted returns.

Chapter Six

Ironing Out
Inefficiencies

—∾—

*Exploiting the Efficient
Market Theory*

*If the efficient markets hypothesis was a publicly traded security,
its price would be enormously volatile.*
> —Andrei Shleifer and Lawrence H. Summers,
> *The Noise Trader Approach to Finance*

IN 1990, ANDREI SHLEIFER AND LARRY SUMMERS mockingly
made the comment that begins this chapter, adding that
the "stock in the efficient markets hypothesis—at least as
it has been traditionally formulated—crashed along with
the rest of the market on October 19, 1987 . . . and its

recovery has been less dramatic than that of the rest of the market."[1] Pretty fun for a pair of economists from Harvard, especially for one who would serve as President Clinton's Secretary of the Treasury and President Obama's Director of the White House National Economic Council.

Why is this important to a *Little Book* about hedge funds? Essentially, hedge funds attempt to exploit the fact that markets are inefficient—it's their bread and butter. Thus, their activity helps drive markets closer to the efficient market theory. For the most part, though, markets have giant inefficiencies that create huge profit opportunities for those who are willing to take some risks. This finding has a huge impact on hedge funds, because in a world of inefficiency there seems to be endless ways to make money and maximize returns. It simply requires the ability to look at things in a different way . . . a contrarian way.

A Kid in a Candy Store

From the time of A.W. Jones until the mid 1980s, the overall sentiment in the marketplace was that hedge fund performance was mainly dictated by luck rather than strategy or skill. Why? The world of finance was operating under Eugene Fama's efficient market theory, which was developed in the 1960s at the University of Chicago.

Here is the gist of it. If markets were rendered efficient, it followed that prices would move in a random pattern, and consequently those who achieved high levels of success would be investors who most quickly acted upon the fundamental news that was available to everybody. In other words, the only thing that moved a stock price was new information; any other changes were random and not predictable. As such, hedge fund managers did not have an edge . . . or did they?

It was April of 1987. I was a first-year law student at Harvard, and desperately wanted to be a summer associate at Goldman Sachs. As I sat in Baker Library, anxiously waiting for my first interview with Goldman Sachs, I picked up *A Random Walk on Wall Street* by Burton Malkiel. It was then that I got my first exposure to the efficient market theory.

Sure, I had heard the term in a Corporate Finance class at Tufts University—my undergraduate alma mater—but the concept barely registered. In plain prose, Professor Malkiel explained that due to perfect information being priced immediately into the markets, the stock prices moved in a random walk. There was no discernible way to predict future prices. Nope. Sorry. No technical analysis, no fundamental analysis, nothing. See, current stock prices were nothing more than a representation of the net present value of the future cash flow streams of each respective company. They were perfectly priced by the market and therefore no one had an edge. If something exogenous happened, well, that would be immediately reflected in price. If you just happened to be on the right side of it, you were the lucky one. You were the monkey on the end of a row of countless monkeys that was flipping a coin and despite the odds it kept coming up heads.

As he put it, "A blindfolded monkey throwing darts at the stock listings could select a portfolio that would do just as well as one selected by experts." In other words, an investor was akin to a monkey in a coin-flipping contest, who—despite the odds—kept getting heads over and over again. This investor's successful stock selection is a fluke as we are fooled by randomness. Malkiel went on to say that since most money managers cannot outperform their respective benchmarks or indexes, they are adding no value; in fact, they may actually be detractors of value as they require transaction costs.

In any case, there I was. Sitting in Baker Library. Waiting for my coveted Goldman Sachs interview. Reading about the efficient market theory. Thinking about its disconnects. And, as it turned out, so were many a more knowledgeable and experienced financial minds.

Times, They Are a Changing

In the late 1980s, Michael Jackson was the King of Pop, Reaganomics was infiltrating the U.S. economy, I was wearing a skinny yellow tie to my Goldman Sachs interview

(I had to get that in there), communism was moments away from heading to the ash heap of history (unless, of course, you are Cuban or North Korean), and we were experiencing the great go-go stock market era, with the market doubling from 1982 to 1987. The world was our oyster and ours for the taking. And then it happened—the financial crash of October 1987. And, just as when a blushing, happy, and blissful newlywed discovers a phone number in her husband's pocket, suddenly everything came into question.

With the stock market in a tailspin, and the economy uncertain and unpredictable, academics—and Fama himself—began to question the existing hypothesis about the market's efficiency. If markets were rendered efficient, they argued, why—after meticulous and often scrupulous analysis—did prices move in patterns? Why on one day was the market one price and then one day later there was a 22.5 percent loss in value? Why were markets rendering themselves not perfectly liquid? Why were sellers who offered a stock at an efficient price unable to find a buyer willing to buy the stock at that efficient price? Why did the equity bubble inflate in the first place?

The answer, my friends, lies in human behavior, which at times appears to contradict economists' expectations of rational beings (same as it did for the newlywed's husband). See, economists often think human beings act rationally, but we know that if anything is predictable, it's the fact that human beings are predictably irrational and unpredictable. Human sentiment effects people's decisions, choices, and behaviors. Like a live performer whose demeanor swings from excited anticipation to paralyzing fear the moment he sets foot on stage, the stock market gyrates based upon human emotions and the impulses of greed and fear. Why?

1. **Investors are not fully rational**. In pursuit of glamour, fortune, and fame or fear of failure, the minds of investors can be clouded by overly emotional thoughts that negatively affect their decision-making abilities.
2. **Investors are overconfident.** They have a tendency to operate under the belief that they are able to pick winning stocks and time the market perfectly. There is no real evidence to support this, but alas market hubris abounds.
3. **Investors, like consumers, are brand snobs**. In thinking that a name brand equals a stellar reputation and stock price movement, investors place huge bets on big name companies that everyone has heard of and often neglect the smaller stocks that outperform them. Apple is the new Microsoft. Imagine that.

In an effort to better describe the market's fluctuations and investors' fickle tendencies, allow me once again to call upon another expert—Benjamin Graham, the father of value investing. He created a fictitious character named Mr. Market to describe the sentiments I echoed above. Somewhat of a manic and over-emotional protagonist, Mr. Market suffers from excessive highs and lows, which interfere with the way in which he does business. The problem—you're his business partner and every day he comes into the office trying to buy your shares or sell his shares of the business based on his mood! On a day when Mr. Market is in a euphoric mood, he demands a high price for his share of the company. At other times, when he is fearful and depressed, you are able to buy the business at severely marked down prices from Mr. Market. And the best part—you can ignore him whenever you want because you know he'll always show up at your office the next morning with a new offer. (Sounds like an over-emotional high school boy in love to me! One day, a dozen roses and the next not even a phone call. Geez!)

The market, you see, is like a barometer of human emotion. Although its underlying value may or may not change, investor behavior often dictates market conditions and consequently affects one's checkbook . . . that is, if you let it. Hedge fund managers, being the contrarian investors that they are, would not just sit there and allow themselves to be the victim of such erratic behavior—especially in moments of crisis like that of Black Monday. Instead, they would discover ways in which to iron out the kinks . . . albeit with a little help from the same academics who told them the market was efficient in the first place!

Living on the Edge

Considered the father of the efficient market theory, Professor Eugene Fama ironically led the charge against it, diving headfirst into a theory that postulated that markets were—you guessed it—*in*efficient. Along with fellow economist Kenneth French, he discovered nonrandom patterns in the market that traders could pounce on to generate positive returns. And as they continued to study the long-term returns from the stock market, their research exposed certain market anomalies that hedge fund managers could exploit in order to correct inefficiencies and produce absolute returns.

1. **Value Stocks vs. Growth Stocks**

Fama and French argued that investors were pouring too much money into *growth stocks* whose values were expected to rise at an above-average rate relative to the market. Generally, these stocks are those that have a presence in the market and are known by investors and noninvestors alike. (Think = Sony and Google.) Contrarily, *value stocks* are those that are generally considered under-valued by the everyday investor and tend to trade at a lower price relative to their fundamentals. (Think = Microsoft or Pfizer—two growth stocks of yesteryear.) These are companies that have strong fundamentals and opportunity sets. In allocating capital to growth stocks rather than value stocks, Fama and French argued that opportunity sets were being misguided and growth was being prohibited.

A quick note—the true magic of any money manager comes from his ability to select the best stocks regardless of outside noise. "It is not a case of choosing those [faces] that, to the best of one's judgment, are really the prettiest, nor even those that average opinion genuinely thinks the prettiest," said John Maynard Keynes, the brilliant economist and legendary investor. "It is for me to ascertain who the other market participants think is the best beauty." Keynes identified the true magic of any money manager; it comes from his ability to select the best stocks. A.W. Jones, Julian Robertson, and Stanley Druckenmiller are often credited as being hedge fund managers who have consistently demonstrated wondrous stock picking ability—long and short ideas. Although they didn't always get it right, their skill primarily comes from steep fundamental analysis. And this is certainly no easy task. If it were simple, everyday traders would be billionaires. There would be a lot more G6s in production and far more extravagant "look at me and how rich I am" birthday celebrations.

2. Small-Company Stocks vs. Large-Company Stocks

Fama and French also found that small-company stocks with low price-to-earnings ratios generally outperformed large-company stocks with high price-to-earnings ratios. As a result, they found that the smaller stocks may turn out to be the better bargain because there is less information about them, contrary to what we would expect in an efficient market.

Julian Robertson, legendary hedge fund manager and founder of Tiger Management, was said to have generated his successful track record by focusing on small companies.

3. Low Beta Stocks vs. Momentum Stocks

Cliff Asness, who had studied under Fama at the University of Chicago, also contributed to Fama's and French's work on ironing out market inefficiencies for profit. Specifically, he conducted a fundamental analysis to determine the true value of a stock and then applied some factors—like momentum—to see if they would influence price movement. He found that *low beta stocks*—stocks whose price movement does demonstrate as much volatility as the overall market—perform better than expected on a risk-adjusted basis.

Asness would later go to Wall Street and start AQR Capital Management in 1997, which would become one of the largest hedge funds in the industry. A brilliant man and all-around nice guy, Asness and his research team developed computer programs that exploited these and other market anomalies. When such anomalies are discovered many rush in to take advantage and then the anomaly no longer exists. It is up to managers like Cliff Asness to continue the search, mining data to uncover the next big, unexploited market treasure.

Fama's and French's findings coincide with the theory of reflexivity, established by George Soros. "The theory of reflexivity can explain such bubbles, while the efficient market hypothesis cannot," he wrote in *The Alchemy of Finance*. According to the hedge fund legend, because the fundamentals of a company were often too complicated to understand, investors often made assumptions and guesstimates about what they perceived to be reality. Consequently, these perceptions and shortcuts changed reality, rendering a feedback loop that caused investors to arrive at a subjective valuation of a stock. In other words, guesses made by investors, forces, or the markets can change the course or arc of outcomes, and money flows can actually change the direction of the future. For example, if an investor made bullish guesstimates about a position, a stock price would rise and the company could improve its performance. Think of the Internet bubble in the late 1990s. It fueled speculation, but the cash thrown in that direction during the speculative fever actually helped to build the industry.

Thus, it naturally followed that markets were not so efficient after all. There was an awful lot of wheel spinning going on in the world of money management. And the effect of this finding on hedge funds was outstanding.

Putting Theory into Practice

As I have mentioned over and over again, hedge funds generate returns by taking advantage of persistent and/or temporary security and asset mispricings and inefficiencies. So, just how do everyday hedge fund managers exploit the market anomalies mentioned above?

Perhaps there is no greater real-life example than George Soros and his bet against the U.S. dollar, which he described as "the killing of a lifetime." In the summer of 1985, Soros believed that currency values in general and the U.S. dollar value in particular were being inefficiently driven up by traders' perceptions, which could reverse at any time. His task—if he chose to accept it—was to determine the timing of such a reversal. And, accept he did. In the late summer of 1985, he shorted the dollar, owning $720 million of other currencies against which the dollar would fall. Luckily, his bet paid off. On September 22, 1985, the Plaza Accord was signed, the dollar was pushed downward, and Soros made an overnight profit of $30 million. Rather than retreat, he doubled down in the belief that investor sentiment and market inefficiency would render his investment profitable. And boy, was he right! By the end of the year, Soros' fund increased by 35 percent, raking in a profit of $230 million.

Although we will be discussing specific strategies that do so in Chapter 7, allow me to call upon SkyBridge's Senior Portfolio Manager and Managing Director Troy Gayeski for some insight and examples. For starters, hedge fund managers may take advantage of micro inefficiencies in markets where small mispricings are apparent. Two simple examples of taking advantage of micro inefficiencies would occur in the following strategies:

1. **Long/Short Equity**: The manager believes a certain stock is too cheap in comparison to a competitor or the broader market. In order to profit from this mispricing, the manager would go long the stock and short the market or the competitor.
2. **Merger Arbitrage Strategy**: If a company is acquiring a smaller competitor in an all-share deal, the manager would short the acquiring company's stock and go long the company to be acquired to

capture the spread between completed acquisition prices and current prices.

Oftentimes, however, hedge funds take advantage of larger macro inefficiencies. A classic example of managers exploiting macro inefficiencies occurred in 2007 when managers took long volatility positions. The macro thesis was fairly straightforward:

- Home prices were already falling rapidly and the subprime market was collapsing.
- Despite assurances from the Fed, the Treasury, Wall Street CEOs (liar, liar, pants on fire), and other powers-that-be that the subprime market and U.S. housing market would be contained, certain managers believed that the pain in housing had to spill over into the broader economy at some point.
- If this occurred, volatility had to escalate from recent cyclical lows. When U.S. home price woes eventually spread to broader capital markets in late 2007 and 2008, long volatility positions generated large profits.

If all of the above examples sound a bit complicated, that's because they are. Don't worry . . . we'll explain these strategies in a bit more detail in Chapter 7. For now, the important takeaway is this: Hedge funds are able to help stabilize markets and take advantage of persistent asset mispricings and market anomalies because markets are in and of themselves inefficient.

The Efficiency of Inefficiency

As I mentioned earlier, many naysayers claimed that early hedge fund managers were able to achieve absolute returns because of luck, luck, and luck. Popular sentiment has dictated that hedge funds were destined to fail because they are operated only by rank speculators. They argue that managers are risky gamblers who are simply interested in speculating on the market and playing roulette with people's money. Yet, these sentiments changed after the financial community—and particularly academics and economists—realized that there were limits to the efficiency of the markets and that money managers could exploit them through systematic research, consistent strategy, and mathematical algorithms that uncovered the discrepancies related to inefficiency.

And yet, the greatest impact of the academic buy-in of inefficient markets was not from the academics themselves but rather from the higher education endowment officers who now saw hedge funds as legitimized and credible cash cows for compound growth. Suddenly, institutions of academic excellence—such as Yale and Harvard—were given the reins to actually invest their endowments and development-earned dollars with hedge funds. As a result, hedge funds began to see a shift in their investor base; no longer were they only used by high-net-worth, wealthy individuals. Institutions wanted a piece of the action, too.

As we learned in Chapter 2, the hedge fund/endowment marriage was led by David Swensen of Yale University, formerly from the bond firm Salomon Brothers and later from the swaps desk at Lehman Brothers. Having stepped into the position to save the dire Yale endowment in 1985, he thought of hedge funds as a good way to diversify the institution's vanilla portfolio—90 percent of which consisted of bonds, stocks, and cash—so as to reduce the portfolio's risk. Plus, if Fama and French were correct in their assertions, hedge fund strategies that produced absolute returns should be easily identifiable.

Initially deterred by the hedge fund fee structure, it took Swensen over five years to invest in the space (Farallon). By 1995, his allocation in hedge funds was at 21 percent with another 31 percent in private equity and real assets. Other institutions quickly followed suit, ultimately leading to a changing of the guard, with institutional investors triggering hedge fund growth after 1987. Ultimately, rendering the uncorrelated returns, which later became known as the "alpha" that hedge funds so longingly desired (hang on . . . we'll get to that in a bit).

The Fact of the Matter . . .

Exploiting efficient market theory has led to explosive profits and predictive capabilities. But the truth of the matter is that there will always be predictive patterns in markets, one of which is that there will always be seemingly unpredictable developments that shock the financial system into a tizzy. Hedge fund managers who are skilled at risk management build these potential episodes into their decision matrices. The manager has a wide range of weapons in his arsenal that can be applied with profitable success at the most bizarre moments and in the most mundane situations. Thus, a hedge fund manager can add real value to a portfolio through thorough research and a proper incisive analysis.

Equally important to exploiting market anomalies is capital preservation. This comes with careful risk management and an understanding that carefully researched and thoughtfully constructed portfolios can and will go wrong. The best managers aren't shooting for the moon, rather, they are taking calculated risks, always with a keen interest in protecting their investors from the look-out-below scenario.

For our current generation of investors it seems as if the world has become more uncertain and less predictable. This is why it has become so compelling to allocate assets toward those who can take advantage of market inefficiencies and reflexivity. No, these managers aren't wearing capes or fancy superhero costumes, but they are applying skill and methodology in the marketplace that gives them an advantage. They are developing hypotheses about positions and fundamentals that other investors overlook and then capitalizing on that contrarian finding.

And such, one thing is certain: There will always be hedge fund managers willing to disprove the efficient market theory and people willing to put their money in an actively managed strategy that aims to disprove it. Even if Boeing were to make a plane that could take off and land itself, many would be skeptical and only ride with a pilot; this will also always be true of money management. So, let's learn the strategies hedge fund managers use to exploit these kinks in the market.

In the Words of a Hedge Fund Legend . . .

Theo Phanoes, CapeView Capital Inc

1. How would you define a hedge fund?

    The defining characteristic of a hedge fund is that it hedges market risk. For example, when a hedge fund buys a mispriced security, in order to capture the Alpha from the convergence of the price to fair value, the hedge fund will short a comparable security that is fairly priced or expensive. To be successful in the long term, a hedge manager needs to be creative, flexible, opportunistic and an opinion leader, not a follower!

2. **How or why did you get started in the industry?**

From a young age I enjoyed debating future events and calculating probabilities, especially business related. After an extensive grounding in finance and markets with a number of banks over an eight-year period, I took the step to start a hedge fund and thereby realize my ambition to invest as a principal.

3. **What hedge fund strategies do you use?**

Our fund is a fundamental credit trading fund, active in markets including high yield bonds, distressed debt, financials and ABS.

4. **What do you see as the future of the industry?**

Alpha is not as scalable as recent growth trends would suggest. Therefore I see two paths for hedge funds:

- **Path 1** will be to remain nimble, opportunistic and compact, maximizing returns in periods of dislocation, and preserving capital during stress.

- **Path** 2 will be to grow larger by diversification into long only and hybrid products. The long only industry has pockets of excellence, but hedge funds competing in this space have good prospects to outperform.

Chapter Seven

A Balancing Act

~

Outperforming the Market while Taking Less Risk

The secret to being successful from a trading perspective is to have an indefatigable and an undying and unquenchable thirst for information and knowledge.

—Paul Tudor Jones

As DISCUSSED THROUGHOUT THIS *Little Book*, hedge funds have a broad mandate and offer investors access to various alternative investment strategies so that they may generate a return that has a low correlation to equity markets. They are able to employ a diverse range of investing strategies so that they can hedge their investments to increase gains and offset losses. The goal is to make sure that under all different types of scenarios the manager can stem losses and generate gains.

This chapter is about the various hedge funds strategies managers use to generate absolute returns regardless of market conditions. Just as there are numerous definitions for hedge funds, there are also various strategy classifications that are further subdivided into different classes. For the purpose of this chapter, we will classify hedge funds in the following four categories (see Figure 7.1):

1. Long/Short Equity
2. Relative Value
3. Event Driven
4. Directional

Figure 7.1   Hedge Fund Strategies

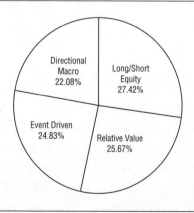

For the purposes of this *Little Book*, I will list the various subdivisions that are classified within each category; however, we will only discuss certain strategies in detail. (As many of these strategies are quite complicated, and some we will not touch upon, I suggest reading *Investment Strategies of Hedge Funds* by Filippo Stefanini for more information on any of the strategies listed in this chapter.)

Long/Short Equity—Borrowing from Peter to Pay Paul

Perhaps the most widely practiced strategy among hedge fund managers is long/short equity, which takes *long* positions in stocks that are expected to rise in value while taking *short* positions in stocks that are expected to decrease in value. The hedge fund manager makes a profit as long as the long position *increases* in value and the short position *decreases* in value *or* the long position outperforms the short position. This practice has become harder and harder to operate as government intervention in markets is making it harder for these sorts of managers to demonstrate their prowess.

What Is Short Selling?

As discussed in the beginning of this *Little Book,* one of the core features that defines hedge funds is short selling. Traditionally, money managers and investors take long positions in a stock, that is, they buy (hopefully undervalued) stocks with the expectation that the stock will increase in value. In simplistic terms, here's how it works: Analyze a company, develop a predictive model on future cash flow streams, and then buy the stocks that you think are undervalued based upon the fundamentals of their future.

Short selling is a completely different beast. Hedge funds managers who exercise the freedom to go short put the investing world in overdrive. By taking short positions in a stock, the manager borrows an overvalued stock from a broker and then sells it with the expectation that it will decline in value. In order to do so, the hedge fund manager must use leverage, that is, he must borrow to buy more of an investment. In this case, the manager is borrowing stock from a prime broker who lends it for a transaction fee—with interest. If successful, the short seller is successful, meaning that there is a price decline. Then the manager buys the same stock back at a lower price than he originally paid for it and returns the borrowed shares to the broker. Magic.

Here's how it works. Let's say that you believe that the stock price of Amaya—a luxury hotel chain—is overvalued at $150 a share. In reviewing its fundamentals, you uncover that its accounts are not what they ought to be. (And, besides, you recently stayed at one of the chain's hotels and your wife made you leave the resort because it was no longer the hotel it was when you vacationed there on your honeymoon 10 years ago!) You call your prime broker, borrow 100 shares of Amaya, and then sell them for $15,000. Within a few months, everyone else is starting to realize that Amaya is overvalued (they must have stayed at the hotel, too!), and the stock price drops to $50 a share. Once again, you call your prime broker, buy the 100 shares back for $7,500, return them to the broker and pocket the difference—$7,500, minus a transaction and interest fee. Easy money, right? Hardly.

A lot can go wrong—with the obvious answer being that you were wrong about Amaya; the hotel gets a much needed makeover; Jennifer Lopez vacations there with her twins, and it becomes the premiere honeymoon destination in the Caribbean—even your wife wants to go back! In this case, the stock rises in value from $150 a share to $250 a share and now you have to buy the 100 shares you borrowed for $25,000, resulting in a $10,000 loss.

This overly simplistic description also neglects to account for external market forces that may dampen the short seller's quest for alpha. What often happens is that others discover what a manager is shorting, and they start buying the stock aggressively in an effort to make the price go up. Effectively, they "squeeze" the manager out of the position. If he is not able to meet his collateral margin call, he will be forced out by his prime broker and suffer a big loss. (Remember, as the price of the stock goes up the manager has to post higher collateral at the prime broker so this will increase buying pressure on the manager if momentum takes over.)

Let's face it, no one grows up (or mostly no one) learning the game from the short side. So, the best way to think about it is in a few different parts.

1. **Detective work**. The real true-blooded hedge fund manager actually finds companies to short. To do so, he must discover something that's deeply wrong with the fundamentals of the company's story so as to ascertain that it is being overvalued in the marketplace. The most effective managers generally target specific companies and designate them for the mortuary or at least the corporate hospital. The individual shorts based on deteriorating fundamentals actually generate better and more meaningful alpha.

2. **Nerves of steel**. As short trades are often crowded and fairly illiquid, it is difficult for the manager to stay in the short if others are spooked and start a buying panic or a classic short squeeze.

3. **Coincidence**. The stock price has to coincide successfully with his assessment of the fundamentals. In other words, the market has to move with his analysis.

4. **Timing**. As the manager is paying interest on the short, the period of depreciation must be closely

monitored. Contrarily, if the stock shoots to the moon and widely trades up, the manager may not be able to post an adequate amount of capital to stay in the short. On the unlevered long side, a manager can stay in the stock for eternity.

The bottom line is that shorting is a tricky strategy. When it works, the manager either makes a handsome profit or has a balanced hedge to the rest of the overall portfolio. The hedge will protect his portfolio from external market conditions and hedge out market risk.

Putting It All Together

As we learned by reading about A.W. Jones, many long/short investors aim to buy underpriced securities and sell expensive securities so that they can push prices to their efficient and relative level. Yet, there are other legendary managers who simply buy securities as they go up and then sell them as they go down. Regardless of the brains behind the long/short equity operation, it is obvious that a manager who can go both long and short has the potential to perform better than a manager who can only go long. Why? A long position + a short position of similar assets consequently neutralizes market risk and results in a low correlation to the market. In other words, the hedge fund manager is able to make a profit from thoughtful stock picking even when the market is overvalued, thus putting the manager's skill at the forefront and the stock market influence on the backburner.

And yet, there is nothing simple about combining the two practices. In fact, if all that was required was just buying some stocks and shorting others, there'd be many a rich man, right?

It all goes back to the lessons learned in the previous chapters—the most effective long/short equity managers seek to exploit the very market anomalies mentioned by Fama and French. Like Julian Robertson, they may buy small company stocks and short large company stock. Like David Einhorn, they may buy value stocks and short growth stocks. Regardless of the method to their madness, there must be a method, a level of expertise, and skill-driven investment decisions. Moreover, these managers must be attuned stock pickers who masterfully, thematically, and thoughtfully select stocks based on their fundamentals.

Now, let's put it all together. . . . The long/short equity manager performs the following actions:

Action 1: Longs (buys) an undervalued stock.
Action 2: Shorts (sells) an overvalued stock.
Goal: Profit from the change in price (spread) between the two stocks.

As such, the long/short equity strategy—even when happily married—is very difficult to practice.

What Comes Up, Sometimes Comes Down

Perhaps one of the greatest short sellers of all time was Julian Robertson, founder of Tiger Capital. Operating in a bull market, he was known to call upon his friends at large investment banks so that he could find the "least favorite child" in their investment portfolio to short.[1] And this investment strategy paid off. Throughout the 1980s, the skeptical manager earned an average of 31.7 percent per year (minus fees), smoking the S&P 500, which earned an average of 12.7 percent during the same time period. For many years shorting was the key ingredient to his success, that is—until the tech bubble burst.

It was 2000. New Year's Eve. As the ball was about to drop in Times Square, cynics prophesized that the new millennium would usher in a technological crisis so catastrophic that it would rival Noah's devastating flood. So serious was this supposed crisis that Federal Reserve Chairman Alan Greenspan spent New Year's Eve in a government crisis center. Yet, Dick Clark rang in 2000 without the smallest glitch. However, the true Y2K crisis affected the long/short equity managers, many of whom were long low P/E stocks and short high P/E Internet stocks.

Robertson was one of those short selling managers. Fed up with the market's irrationality, he closed his fund in late March 2000. In a letter to investors that year, the then-67-year-old blamed the fund's shortfall on the Internet bubble. "As you have heard me say on many occasions, the key to Tiger's success over the years has been a steady commitment to buying the best stocks and shorting the worst," he wrote. "In a rational environment, this strategy performs well. But in an irrational market, where earnings and price considerations take a back seat to mouse clicks and momentum, such logic, as we have learned, does not count for much."[2] This hedge fund legend was vindicated when shortly after he shut his fund, the Internet bubble collapsed. Prices on the NASDAQ peaked on March 10, 2000, at 5048.62, then the bubble burst and prices declined by as much as 60 percent with many publicly traded high fliers going bankrupt.

(A quick aside—perhaps in a testament to Mr. Robertson's stellar stock picking abilities and business acumen, he spawned a cluster of hedge fund superstars who went on to start their own funds. Known as Tiger Cubs, many of these managers have posted spectacular performance and can trace their start to the ways and wisdom of Julian.)

Likewise the long/short equity strategy faces similar challenges in today's economy. Although John Paulson

achieved spectacular profits by shorting subprime mort-
gages and indexes in 2008, he achieved equally disastrous
results in 2011 using the same investment strategy. While
making a reflation bet that financials and other economy-
related stocks would rise in concert with an improving
U.S. economy, Mr. Paulson got the timing wrong and
suffered 35 to 40 percent losses.

Shit happens. Robertson and Paulson have gotten a
lot more right than wrong; however, their high-profile stories demonstrate the perils and risks associated with
shorting. Moreover, these unfortunate failures confirm
that short sellers at hedge funds cannot manipulate
markets.

Relative Value—Two of a Kind . . . but Different

Relative value strategies are "arbitrage transactions" that
seek to profit from the spread between two positions
rather than from the general market direction.[3] Referred
to as "pair" trading, relative value managers invest in a
pair of highly correlated securities. They search for discrepancies in the values of closely related securities (securities that tend to move in the same direction at the same
time) so that they may take advantage of price differentials
by simultaneously buying and selling them. In other words,
pair traders search for situations where two companies in
the same industry—or even two companies in different

industries—may move in opposite directions. As a result of this practice, investors profit from the "relative value" of the two securities.

Strategies within this classification include:

- Convertible Bond Arbitrage
- Fixed-Income Arbitrage
- Equity Market Neutral

Relative value funds can pair trade indices, futures, options, currencies, and commodities; however, stocks that are in the same industry and have similar trading histories are most often used in this strategy. In my humble opinion, the pairs trading process is one of the most fascinating forms of hedge fund investing; however, it may also be the most nuanced. Part art and part science, the process requires a skilled manager to sift through securities in an attempt to find those that may have similar things in common, but move in opposite directions and/or are complementary to each other if they are tied together in a business transaction.

For example, let's say a hedge fund manager is an expert in the health care industry. In looking at the balance sheet and growth characteristics of Wyeth and Pfizer, he notices that Wyeth has strong fundamentals and is worried about the related expenses and future of Pfizer.

As such, he buys Wyeth while shorting Pfizer. The outcome of his decision will depend solely on whether the manager was correct in his research and decision; it will have no bearing on the pharmaceuticals market as a whole.

Here's how it works: the relative value manager identifies two positions—Position A and Position B—that are in the same industry and have similar trading histories. When Position A *rises* in value and Position B *falls* in value, the relative value manager *buys* Position A and *shorts* Position B. When Position A and B converge in price again, he closes the trade and makes a profit. If the trade goes extremely well, the manager will book a profit on both sides—both Positions A and B. This rarely happens. More often than not, both positions will move together.

Although hedge fund managers are supposed to be able to generate absolute returns regardless of market conditions, relative value strategies are most effective in a sideways market, that is, a market that is neither rising nor falling but trading within a specific range. As such, they generally have little or no directional market exposure to the underlying equity or bond market. In desultory markets, the individual analysis might be in a better position to shine through.

Of course, it's not as easy as it sounds. Relative value strategies require the manager to have both extensive knowledge of the individual positions *and* the market.

Arbitrage

Before we delve into the individual relative value strategies, we must first define arbitrage. Arbitrage is a financial transaction that involves two similar items that are priced differently in different markets. In practice, the trader simultaneously purchases a position in one market and sells the similar position in a different market at a different price. In other words, he is exploiting the price differences of identical positions by buying the same security at a lower price and selling it right away at a higher price. In a perfect scenario, the arbitrageur profits from a difference in the price between the two and earns an immediate profit with no market risk. For example, an announced deal might provide an opportunity for risk arbitrage, or the issuance of a convertible bond by a publicly traded company may signal an opportunity for convertible arbitrage. In the world of high-yield bond investing, getting long the bond and short the underlying stock is known as capital structure arbitrage investing (we'll get to these terms in just a bit).

Perhaps the most famous arbitrage desk in the world was created by Gus Levy at Goldman Sachs. Predecessors to Gus included L.J. Tenenbaum, Robert E. Rubin (a former U.S. Secretary of Treasury—one of the best,

I might add), Richard Perry, Thomas Steyer, Edward Lampert, Daniel Och, Frank Brosens, and Eric Mindich. The process of investing that was developed at Goldman Sachs has been the foundation of all sorts of arbitrage strategies. The basis of such investing: Buy one security, short the other, and capture the spread. Or it could involve identifying a price difference in the same security or asset in different markets and flipping the inventory to capture the spread.

Here's how it works. A trader notices a difference between the price of HSBC on the New York Stock Exchange (NYSE) and Hong Kong Stock Exchange, where it is selling for $49.05 and $49.25, respectively. A skillful arbitrageur would quickly purchase HSBC on the NYSE and then sell it on the Hong Kong Exchange. After transaction costs of a penny each way, there is a risk-free profit of 18 cents. People become billionaires from this sort of stuff; however, as more people enter the market this strategy's spreads start to narrow. (The decimalization of NASDAQ trading went a long way toward narrowing spreads.)

Investors beware: In turbulent times, arbitrage strategies can be dangerous. The price division seemingly there today can evaporate instantaneously with all of the flash trading and technology that have entered the system.

Convertible Arbitrage

Let's start small. A convertible security is a hybrid security that can be *converted* into a common stock or bond at a predetermined time and price. In possessing the features of both a stock and a bond, the investor is able to either hold the bond or convert it to a stock if he anticipates that its price will rise in value. Think of it as a bond with an embedded call option into the stock. At some point (depending on the stock price), the bond holder has the right to exercise into the stock at a predetermined price.

Convertible arbitrage is the long-lost cousin of the long/short equity investing strategy in that it takes a *long* position in a company's convertible security (stock/bond hybrid) that is expected to rise in value while simultaneously taking a *short* position in the same company's stock. In doing so, the investor seeks to profit on the price difference between the convertible bond relative to the company's actual stock.

Here's how it works:

- Big Bang Company issues a convertible bond.
- The hedge fund manager buys the convertible bond *and* shorts the Big Bang Company's stock.
- If the stock price *falls*, the manager makes a profit from its short position.

- If the stock price *rises*, the manager's position is hedged because the bond is *converted* into a stock.

Sounds like a win-win situation, right? Don't get too excited. This strategy is not without its flaws. For starters, convertible bonds are subject to holding patterns whereby the manager is required to hold them for a specified period of time before he can convert them into a stock. As a result, convertible arbitrageurs often are victims of the unpredictable and frequently turbulent market. There have also been periods of time where these trades are very overcrowded, and the tighter spreads require people to use leverage to try to boost their returns. This type of leverage can add volatility and greater uncertainty.

Equity Market Neutral

Equity market neutral hedge fund managers make "concentrated bets" by taking long and short positions in stocks that have a perceived level of pricing convergence. As the name implies, this long/short equity strategy variation is "market neutral," that is, its performance is not correlated to the movements of the market. Yet, unlike long/short equity strategies, this strategy bears higher levels of systemic risk.

More specifically, equity market neutral strategies seek to exploit differences in stock prices within the same sector or industry so that they may minimize their exposure to the systemic risk of the stock market. Ultimately, the goal is to achieve a beta as close to zero as possible, in other words, eliminate risk and be profitable regardless of market conditions.

Equity market neutral is a very difficult strategy to implement because it heavily relies on regression data and past movements of securities. Specifically, managers who utilize this strategy are constantly analyzing price patterns to determine which securities move with uncorrelated adjustments to the market. For example, the manager will buy mortgage-backed security paper that will generate yield and therefore have price support despite the forces of stock market gyration. They may then short the ABX index, which are the derivative contracts related to mortgage subprime volatility. If things go wrong, there is an effective hedge; if things go right, a profit is made less the price of the insurance that was put on in the pairing. As you can see, the actual movement of the market barely matters because the gains and losses offset one another.

Unlike the other strategies we have discussed, equity market neutral strategies have less associated risk because managers attempt to place specialized bets on price convergence. That said, it can go haywire when more leverage is applied.

Event Driven—One Man's Loss Is Another Man's Gain

As the name implies, event-driven strategies attempt to capitalize on opportunities that occur within a company and exploit pricing anomalies that result from a specific event. Oftentimes, these strategies occur before or after a merger or acquisition (hence the name merger arbitrage), bankruptcy, buyout, or spin-off. In this instance, a hedge fund manager takes a significant position in a limited number of companies with *special* situations—and by special I mean unusual situations that provide money-making opportunities.

Event-driven strategies can be further subdivided into the following:

- Merger Arbitrage
- Distressed Securities

■ ■ ■

In 1985, Tom Steyer—a former Goldman Sachs compatriot who escaped the hustle and bustle of Wall Street in favor of San Francisco—started Farallon and created the event-driven fund. Just as he practiced at his alma mater, Steyer's day began by studying the merger and acquisition action taking place across the continent so that he could pounce on the stock's initial price offering before it skyrocketed after the takeover bid was announced. If he discovered that a merger or acquisition was about to occur, he would quickly compare the current trading price per share to the bid price. In knowing that the current trading price would move toward the direction of the bidding price if the deal went through, he would buy the stock and short the acquiring firm so that he could pocket the difference if the acquisition was consummated.

Here's how it works. Imagine that you are a manager of an event-driven hedge fund. While sipping your iced espresso and reading *DealBreaker*, you discover that Wolfeer Cosmetics is going to be acquired by Little Red Lipsticks. At the time of the announcement, Wolfeer's stock had been trading at $10, however, Little Red Lipsticks bid $20 a share and you think it might move up to $16. In thinking that the deal is going to reach fruition, you snap up your shares. If the merger is successful, you would pocket an additional $4 per share. If, however, the merger does not occur, you would lose $6 per share. No risk, no reward.

As you can see, event-driven strategies require extensive knowledge and skill so that a hedge fund manager can determine if the deal will actually occur. The hedge fund manager must be able to clearly identify the event and systematically analyze the potential acquisition so that

A BALANCING ACT   [137]

he can determine the feasibility of it actually occurring. To do so, he must take into consideration news reports, access to company records, and/or potentially publicly disclosed contracts that explain the agreement, merger, or spin-out. He must also analyze the overall state of the industry—the correlations of stocks within the industry and the industry's correlation to the overall market. This exhaustive approach will help the manager better assess deal risk.

But what, you ask, can possibly block the event-driven manager on his quest for financial glory? The government, antitrust regulators, a shareholder revolution, a possible new buyer, a relentless company—all the players that make up the nightmares of our typical event-driven manager. You get the picture. These are factors that most hedge fund managers cannot control.

Although event-driven strategies use very little leverage and historically provided alpha, their moment in the spotlight has surely faded. Why? Event-driven strategies—specifically merger arbitrage—tend to have a higher correlation to the overall market than other hedge fund strategies. Think about it—this is strategy that earns its bread and butter based on mergers and acquisitions, which tend to happen more successfully in a thriving economy. It's no wonder that this strategy has been underperforming since the 2007 to 2009 economic crisis.

Moreover, many mergers and acquisitions do not go as planned. For example, if the announced deal doesn't go through or is blocked by the government, being short the acquirer and long the acquisition target may reverse direction on the manager and cause losses. The manager may own out of the money put and call option, respectively, to hedge and protect against a busted deal.

Directional

Directional strategies take advantage of global market trends and make leveraged bets. Unlike the strategies just discussed, these strategies do not provide a hedge against market risk; rather they seek to preserve capital and earn absolute returns by taking advantage of global market trends and the direction of movements in the financial market. Strategies within this classification include:

- Global Macro Funds
- Managed Futures

Global Macro Funds

When I think of the global macro hedge fund managers, I always seem to imagine the same scenario: a group of contrarians, pacing back and forth in a war room as they try to assess every price movement that is going on in real time around the planet. Interest rate movements, commodity prices, currencies, stocks, and bonds—basically everything on the Earth that trades!

Global macro funds are akin to investing without limits; they can invest in any market, trade any asset class, and use any financial instrument. Using a top-down approach, they attempt to anticipate macroeconomic trends and price changes on capital markets by analyzing the variables associated with the different countries in which they allocate their capital. To do so, they study how certain political events, global macroeconomic factors, and financial fundamentals influence the prices of securities, indices, options, futures contracts, and so on. Simultaneously, they analyze both developed and emerging markets worldwide and the risk/return potential of a given investment.[4] Once they determine a global investment thesis, they make leveraged bets on the direction of the movements in the market and earn the difference between the borrowing cost and the profit from their directional bets going the way that they predict.

Although global macro strategies are different from the strategies created by A. W. Jones, they are credited with putting hedge funds on the map. Perhaps the most famous trade in hedge fund history occurred in 1992 when George Soros' Quantum Fund "broke the Bank of England" and then—in a different but similar trade—brought the Italian lira to its knees by selling short an enormous amount of both countries' currencies. The result: the demise of the pound and the lira from the European Monetary System; a profit of $2 billion dollars for Soros; and the emergence of hedge funds in everyday vernacular.

Ultimately, the success of this strategy is dependent upon the skill and insight of the global macro managers who seek to preserve capital by correctly anticipating price movements. Macro funds—like Long/Short equity managers—are suffering in an age of central bank intervention. At some point, this sort of intervention will end and this strategy will be able to flourish again.

In the Words of a Hedge Fund Legend . . .

Deepak Narula, Managing Partner, Metacapital Management

1. How would you define a hedge fund?

   A hedge fund is a loosely regulated investment partnership with a more sophisticated investor base relative to traditional long only strategies. Hedge funds use long-short strategies and leverage. Shorting helps to "hedge" market risks, while leverage helps to magnify the difference in price changes between longs and shorts.

2. **How or why did you get started in the industry?**

It was a logical extension of doing research and positioning proprietary ideas on the sell side.

3. **What hedge fund strategies do you use?**

We engage in active trading strategies in long-short relative value trades. These strategies focus on alpha generation. We also take sector betas that are attractively priced and hard to source in a typical long only structure.

4. **What do you see as the future of the industry?**

The future for active management is quite bright. Given the low absolute level of interest rates, fixed income returns will remain quite low, while the high volatility and lack of directionality in equity markets make long only strategies less effective. However, managers who mainly take a long only strategy and call it a hedge fund to justify higher fees may see attrition of assets. The market will pay up for real alpha and superior risk management, and is increasingly able to differentiate those from "dressed up" long only strategies.

Chapter Eight

If You Can't Beat 'Em, Join 'Em

—✺—

Hedge Fund Manager Selection and Due Diligence

In evaluating people, you look for three qualities: integrity, intelligence, and energy. And if you don't have the first, the other two will kill you.

—Warren Buffett

THROUGHOUT THIS BOOK I have been stressing the key differences between hedge funds and other asset classes. In an effort to generate absolute returns and produce alpha, a hedge fund manager must possess the uncanny ability to fundamentally select the best stocks and systematically diversify his portfolio so that he can produce risk-adjusted returns. But for every stock-picking guru like David Einhorn or Dan Loeb there are dozens of other nameless hedge fund managers who are not quite as successful.

Although the purpose of this book is not to uncover the secret formula for achieving alpha-like return, nor is it to explain in painstaking detail how to invest in hedge funds, this chapter will spend a bit of time showing you how investors and fund of hedge fund managers screen the over 9,000 hedge funds that are currently in operation.

The core to this hedge fund investment process is:

- Manager Selection
- Portfolio Construction

As hedge fund managers are like snowflakes with no two being alike, they all have very different pedigrees, philosophies, processes, strategies, track records, and personalities—all of which is important to assess when making an allocation decision. Although the discovery, evaluation, and monitoring processes detailed in this chapter can appear a bit daunting, they are essential in screening hedge fund managers so that you can identify the appropriate person to manage your hedge fund allocation.

Stop Right There!

Before we get down and dirty, a few notes. . . .

Although I have mentioned it before, it bears a bit of repeating—hedge fund investing is not for everyone . . . nor is it an accessible option for many. As many would say, the industry should come with a surgeon general's warning: *Investing without proper due diligence or proper personal risk assessment can be bad for your financial (and mental) health. Do your homework. Be prepared. Have a proper screen. Research. Research. Research.*

As with any other investment, one must first clearly define one's goals and objectives before allocating capital to a hedge fund. As I also said at the beginning of this *Little Book*, hedge funds are not for everyone nor are they a substitute for other investment vehicles. For the majority of people—or anyone who doesn't have 1 or 2 million dollars that they are willing to invest—mutual funds, with a swirl of alternative asset exposure is probably the best option. So, if you meet the criteria of an accredited investor and believe that an allocation to hedge funds will better diversify your portfolio so that you can generate risk-adjusted returns, I suggest that you proceed with caution.

Also, be sure you have a threshold for pain and fully ascribe to the philosophy that slow and steady wins the race. In the investing world—especially the alternative investment and hedge fund world—you should always expect the unexpected. You should also always assume that things can—and usually do—go wrong. Hedge funds, after all, can collectively have good and bad times. For example, in 2002 hedge funds were viewed as heroes as they were only down 1.5 percent while U.S. equities were down 23 percent. Conversely, in 1998 hedge funds were the goats as they were only up 2.6 percent, while U.S. equities were up 26.7 percent. As such, if you would like to invest in hedge funds, keep in mind two things:

1. Hedge funds are not a panacea for all the world's ills.
2. Hedge funds exist not only to generate attractive and competitive absolute returns, they also have to manage downside risk and have lower volatility than broader markets. Furthermore, they have to do so with as low of a correlation to broader markets as possible.

All this being said, any skilled and vetted manager who has a relative investment thesis should see his portfolio perform well on an absolute and risk-adjusted basis over time.

Lastly, while the tips I provide in this chapter will never be sufficient on their own to enable an investor to make 100-percent-for-sure decisions, nor will they guarantee that an investor will generate enough wealth to buy a mansion in the Hamptons, they will help an investor make an informed and smart investment decision. And, who knows? They just might afford you the funds to fly your girlfriend to Paris at a moment's notice . . . just go easy on the expensive champagne.

Manager Selection

If the role of the hedge fund manager is one of skill as he seeks to produce absolute returns and generate alpha, then it follows that an investor must choose a skillful hedge fund manager, one who is able to produce uncorrelated returns through skillful and active stock picking. As I mentioned in the previous chapters, I am not naïve enough to suggest that this is 100 percent possible; for every Julian Robertson there are 50 aspiring boy wonders who ultimately meet their financial demise in their quest for alpha. However, hedge fund manager selection is crucial in reaching your investment objectives and your portfolio's success. Thus, our journey into the hedge fund process begins with manager selection—a lengthy process where an investor determines the quality of the hedge fund manager, his staff, and his business practices by a thorough due diligence process that requires extensive research, monitoring, and analysis (we'll get to that term in a few moments).

Although manager selection might appear to be a rather tedious process, it is perhaps the most crucial element of the hedge fund investment process. And yet, given the historical lack of transparency plus the high level of complexity that surrounds the industry, it is often difficult for investors to access the information needed to make these decisions.

As we learned in Chapter 6, the market is riddled with inefficiencies that managers must exploit so that they may find trades where the upside potential appears greater than the downside risk. It is the job of skillful hedge fund managers to identify these market inefficiencies, recognize the clandestine opportunities they afford, and then exploit these anomalies to protect capital and generate risk-adjusted returns for their investors. As such, the skilled money manager—or hedge fund team—is one who conducts fundamental, quantitative, and qualitative investment analysis, selects the appropriate asset mix, and monitors risks on an ongoing basis.

Some critics would have you think that hedge fund managers are nothing more than risk-loving gamblers who are only interested in speculating on the market and playing roulette with other people's money. Our research and portfolio management team at SkyBridge has seen firsthand that the world's finest hedge fund managers are not lucky monkeys flipping coins. Rather, they are great odds makers who use the powers of statistical, fundamental, and qualitative analysis to come up with the next market winners. And the best have an edge—better analysis, predictive modeling, and superior risk management that can replicate exemplary performance. The edge basically means that they see things differently from others in the overall market; they can move in contrarian ways but also be confident enough to move with the market and not fight the flow of momentum. Make money, join the crowd when necessary, but be bold enough to cut against it when the time is right. It is here in these very trenches that riches are made and clients satisfied.

The Screening Process

So, how do you find these managers? Sharpen your pencils . . . it's time to do your due diligence.

At SkyBridge Capital, we have a lengthy manager selection process that focuses on investment research and due diligence as well as operational due diligence. To make a long story short, the investment research and due diligence process is focused on determining or not a manager can:

- Generate attractive absolute and relative returns.
- Manage risk.
- Produce uncorrelated returns, with relatively attractive liquidity.
- Evolve as market conditions evolve.

Perhaps most important, we have to understand how they will behave when the shit hits the fan in market debacles like LTCM, September 11th, the summer of 2002, 2008, the European financial crisis, and so on.

To give you a more thorough understanding of how to conduct this investment research and due diligence, allow me to call upon Troy Gayeski, SkyBridge Capital's senior portfolio manager, who breaks down the process into the following categories:

- **Pedigree**: Pedigree is an all-encompassing term we use to assess whether a manager possesses the right experience and skill to execute a particular strategy in a particular market environment. Typically, an investor should strive to find a manager with many years of real "buy-side experience," that is, the manager should have actually managed a reasonable amount of capital over a reasonable period of time. The exception to this rule is a new, cutting-edge manager who is implementing strategies that may not have existed three years ago.

    You would be surprised at how many hedge funds fail the basic "experience" test. For instance, if a manager's only prior experience is that he was a fixed-income salesman, you could undoubtedly find someone with more relevant experience and skills.

For whatever reason, a lot of hedge fund investors tend to be drawn like moths to a flame to big-name sell-side guys who come out and launch a new hedge fund. A general rule of thumb: Avoid these guys like the plague as history has shown that they tend to always fail. After all, managing capital for private investors is completely different from running market making/prop trading outfits.

Pedigree also includes a manager's temperament and qualitative judgment. Is he a loose cannon or thoughtful and deliberative? Has he experienced personal and professional setbacks in his career and how has he responded? Has he treated his investor capital with prudence or has he viewed it as a tool to make a name for himself and get rich quick?

Answering these questions takes a lot of work. But, if you want to invest with a hedge fund manager you have to be willing to roll up your sleeves and analyze that manager's pedigree.

- **Opportunity Set**: Opportunity Set is a term used to describe whether a manager and a strategy are taking advantage of a compelling market inefficiency. At SkyBridge, one of our favorite phrases is "You can't get blood from a stone." In other words, if there is no opportunity in the market to generate attractive returns, then a manager's pedigree and/or track record is irrelevant. After all, you don't want to work with a manager who has to be Superman and the Green Lantern all rolled into one as his chance of making money is diminished.

Real-time predictive opportunity set analysis is one of the hardest things for hedge fund investors to iteratively get correct because of the dynamic nature of markets. The lazy man looks at a great track record and extrapolates it into infinity. The wise man looks at market inefficiencies and determines where the next 12 to 18 months' low-hanging fruit resides.

- **Alpha Proposition**: Alpha proposition encompasses the value that a manager adds to a strategy above and beyond the strategy or market beta. This value can include better modeling techniques, better trade structuring to enhance risk versus reward, strategic shifts in asset class/security exposure, or a greater understanding of how the evolving macro environment may affect this strategy. Think about it from the standpoint of your pocketbook: If you are paying 2 percent and 20 percent, you may as well make sure you are getting the greatest added value possible.

- **Fundamental Risk of Loss**: Fundamental risk of loss means exactly what it says. What is the range of risk of loss you can expect if the manager's underlying positioning is just flat wrong? Clearly, the lower, the better.

- **Volatility Profile**: Volatility profile refers to the fluctuation in value an investor can expect as the manager plays out his investment thesis. In order to generate returns, some level of volatility must be accepted. However, certain managers exhibit higher degrees of volatility than others. As such, investors must fully assess a manager's volatility profile before investing with him.

- **Correlation Properties**: Correlation properties refer to a manager's correlation behavior to broader asset classes and/or other managers. As discussed in Chapter 6, the lower the fundamental correlation, the better.

- **Convergence Risk**: Remember the 1987 crash, collapse of Long Term Capital Management, or the economic crisis of 2007 to 2009? Many managers—who were not correlated to the market—lost their breakfasts . . . and much more. That is convergence risk. Managers are aware of this phenomenon and must have strategies in place that will mitigate extreme downside risk and make money in extreme market crises. Most hedge fund strategies, unfortunately, suffer from some degree of convergence risk—it just comes with the territory. That said, most hedge funds' convergence risk is far below that of mutual funds.

- **Liquidity Profile**: The liquidity profile of a manager is extremely important to assess for a variety of reasons. As discussed in Chapter 1, liquidity is important because it provides managers with the ability to evolve as the market environment evolves while also allowing them to change their minds when they deem fit.

  Furthermore, a satisfactory liquidity profile is a necessary ingredient in allowing managers to pay back their clients in the event of redemptions. As a general rule investors should not see managers with asset/liability mismatches, which lead to gating and suspensions of redemptions. On the other hand, investors should not see managers who offer ridiculously onerous liquidity terms to clients when they could clearly offer more generous terms given the strategy being pursued.

- **Empirical Evidence to Triangulate Theory**: Theories are like assholes—everyone's got one. As such, managers need empirical evidence—in the form of fundamental and quantitative market, strategy, and manager data—to back up their conceived investment theses. Investors must pore over track records and market data in order to better understand how managers execute their strategies in various market environments. This data will also help investors better anticipate how their managers will behave in various future scenarios.

A quick note—do not put too much emphasis on statistical techniques. As history has proven, statistical and quantitative techniques have done far more harm than good to both capital markets and hedge fund investors (think LTCM). It's hard to convince yourself that levering any investment strategy 100:1 is safe unless you are both egregiously arrogant and have developed such sophisticated models that nothing can go wrong. After all, what good is a Sharpe Ratio of 4 for three years when you lose 100 percent of your money in the fourth year? That said, the application of data analysis can be helpful when applied by thoughtful, humble minds.

The operational due diligence process is focused on making sure the manager does not or *cannot* do anything completely stupid on the business side to blow up his business. Remember, most hedge fund blowups have occurred due to operational issues not bad investment bets (think Madoff or Beacon Hill). As we like to say at SkyBridge, a manager has to follow the Hippocratic Oath of investing: "First do no harm." In other words, you must be as certain as possible that operational risk is extremely low before you invest in the hedge fund. Operational due diligence may be broken up into the following categories:

- **Valuation**: At SkyBridge Capital, we focus like hawks on how a manager's portfolio is valued and have insisted upon independent confirmation of portfolio net asset value. Having independent portfolio valuation policies is critical for removing the conflict of interest that results because of a hedge fund's fee structure. It always ends in tears for the managers (and consequently all of their clients) who start marking to their own fantasy and do not use mark-to-market pricing methodologies as a reality check for their investment theses . . . just ask Beacon Hill or Plainfield investors.

- **Cash Flow Controls**: Investors must always make sure that there are many checks and balances in place between the manager and his service providers (prime broker and custodian) for wiring money in and out of his fund. If all of your hedge fund manager's ducks are in a row, you won't have to worry as much if he goes rouge because he won't have the ability to make it to Zimbabwe or New Zealand with your money (just ask people who invested with Madoff or Bayou how important this can be).

- **Trade Processing**: Trade processing ensures proper segregation of duties between front office (i.e., traders and PMs) and mid-back office (i.e., operations and accounting) so that any mischief by traders can be significantly mitigated or avoided.

- **Quality of Service Providers**: Investors also need to make sure that managers are utilizing high-quality service providers for custodial, prime brokerage, audit, and administration services that pursue industry best practices. At the end of the day, you want to make sure that each of these service providers is providing high-quality oversight so as to mitigate business risk.

- **Counterparty Risk**: The main focus for counterparty risk typically resides in lending relationships where a prime broker provides modest amounts of leverage to help amplify a hedge fund's returns. Unfortunately, Wall Street has a reputation for being a cutthroat place for a very good reason: It is. Thus, investors need to make sure that hedge funds have appropriate standards in place to protect them when their counterparties get squirrelly in convergence events. On a more sophisticated note, counterparty risk is also important when evaluating over-the-counter instruments. In other words, you never want to get into a situation where the counterparty does not honor its contractual obligations because it goes bust. (Think = Lehman Brothers.)

- **General Business Risk**: There are a wide variety of general business risk issues that an investor must address. Perhaps one of the most important is investor concentration. As a general rule, it is better to see hedge funds with a diversified client mix as it helps to mitigate the risk associated with one large investor who may get into trouble.

The Never-Ending Process

As per the Investors' Committee of the President's Working Group on Financial Markets of 2009, due diligence is defined as "the process of gathering and evaluating information about a hedge fund manager prior to investing in order to assess whether a specific hedge fund is an appropriate choice for the portfolio." It combines qualitative research and quantitative analysis in order to assess the manager's—and his team's—character, investment style/approach, and historical/current performance relative to the market.

Not only may manager selection—vis-à-vis due diligence— be the most important stop in our race to find the most appropriate hedge fund manager, but it may also be the most tedious and labor-intensive. After all, who has time to sift through database upon database of hedge funds? Who has the skills to properly assess a fund's performance? (Fortunately, there is a cure—fund of funds—but we'll get to that a bit later.)

So, just how does one go about identifying and assessing a hedge fund manager and his associated levels of risk? Although there is not a due diligence Bible or a one-size-fits-all approach, we suggest employing a robust due diligence program with the following or similar scope and process. Although I toyed with including this sample program directly in this *Little Book*, its value and relevancy is essential for an investor's manager selection process. So, without further ado, please refer to the appendix at the end of this book to see a due diligence questionnaire, which was provided by Managing Director and our Head of Operational Due Diligence Ken McDonald.

Alternatively, investors may choose to consult a "well-tailored due diligence questionnaire (DDQ)" so that they may better understand a hedge fund's opportunities and risks. According to the Investors' Committee of the President's Working Group on Financial Markets, the DDQ "should contain probing questions regarding the material aspects of a hedge fund's business and operations" and cover the items listed above.

A word of caution: As investors all have different objectives and monetary limitations, investors are strongly urged to pursue multiple exploratory processes so that they can better tailor their discovery process to hedge fund managers being considered. Our goal at SkyBridge is to find managers who can fit into an overall asset allocation and portfolio that will generate a combined, low double-digit return consistently through a long-term market cycle.

Filling in the Data

Just how do you find the information needed to begin the hedge fund manager discovery?

Given the marketing and solicitation restrictions imposed upon hedge funds by regulatory agencies, word-of-mouth referrals remain the flavor of choice when gathering information on hedge fund managers and their investments. Another source of information is seminars or conferences where hedge fund managers and economists provide potential investors with information. You may even want to consider attending an alternatives conference such as the SkyBridge Alternatives (SALT) Conference, where you can expose yourself to some of the greatest hedge fund minds in the industry and learn about best practices and investing strategies within the context of a dynamic and turbulent economy. Lastly, I urge anyone who is interested in investing in hedge funds to read, read, read. Read about the industry in the newspaper, or on the web, or in books like this one.

Once you have obtained some general knowledge about the industry and particular managers, you must dig a bit deeper so that you can satisfactorily respond to your due diligence questionnaire. The best way to gather this type of data on a hedge fund is to obtain its offering memorandum, disclosure documents, and legal partnership form. From these documents you will be able to learn about the fund's minimum investment, management fee plus incentive fee, investment strategy, lockup and redemption period, provisions for withdrawal, and so forth. A word of caution: If a manager is reluctant to provide you with this information—RUN!

Portfolio Construction

According to the Alternative Investment Management Association's (AIMA) Roadmap to Hedge Funds, "The essence of portfolio construction is to utilize all available opportunities to diversify risk and use available optionality to hedge unwanted risk." As such, hedge fund managers generally balance bottom-up manager selection with top-down thematic/strategy diversification when construct-ing a typical portfolio.

A top-down investing approach requires managers to accurately forecast macroeconomic conditions, ascertain their investment implications, and correctly interpret their impact on various sections of the overall market, particu-lar industries, and specific companies. Sounds intense! So, allow me to translate. If you plan on working for a hedge fund then you need to take a thorough deep-dive approach to your individual security analysis, assessing upside and downside cases as well as understanding how the security selection fits into the overall portfolio. If you are looking to invest, you need to make sure the manager is doing this sort of rigorous work with his team of analysts.

On the other hand, a bottom-up investing approach requires managers to thematically identify individual investment opportunities through fundamental analysis so that they may tactically allocate the assets in the portfolio. Described as a buy a dollar for fifty cents strategy, this approach requires the manager to have the discipline to wait until valuable bargains emerge and the patience to stick with those investments until value is realized. Perhaps more importantly, the manager must also possess a contrarian mind that urges him to hold a position regard-less of the prevailing direction of the market or his own views about the global economy. Lastly, he must be nimble—that is, he must be able to reverse the investment decision if appropriate. Sounds complicated? It is. As an entire book can be written on this subject, I encourage you to read *The Intelligent Investor* by Benjamin Graham and Warren Buffett.

Stay Alert . . . It's Your Money

Although you have selected the hedge fund manager or team of managers, your work is not over. As I always tell my colleagues—do not rest on your laurels. Now is the time to monitor your hedge fund manager, investment, and performance.

On a monthly or quarterly basis, investors must monitor their manager and portfolio to review the effectiveness and consistency of the strategy. At SkyBridge we suggest a constant process of triangulation, which involves ongoing review of the following . . . once again provided to you courtesy of Troy Gayeski:

- **Opportunity Set Evolution**: Oftentimes an opportunity set begins to wane faster than anticipated and it's time to hit the eject button.
- **Risk Reports/Portfolio Positioning**: Iteratively reviewing a manager's portfolio positioning can give an investor great insight into how the manager is evolving as market conditions evolve. It can

also demonstrate that the manager is straying into markets and strategies that his skill set does not support.

- **Personnel Changes**: Frequent staff changes can be an early warning sign that a hedge fund is going to lose essential decision makers. So, keep a finger on the pulse of that employee roster!

- **Performance Review**: Reviewing a manager's ongoing performance—with expectations and peers—can give great insight into whether a manager is properly executing his strategy and appropriately managing risk. Investors must pay careful attention to both underperformance and outperformance to make sure a manager is not taking too much risk or exhibiting style drift. Let's face it—no matter how compelling an investment thesis or manager is in theory, if he cannot generate attractive returns, who cares what the theory states?

- **Future Market Expectations**: Having ongoing dialogue with the manager concerning how he anticipates the market environment and his portfolios to evolve under various conditions is critical for managing expectations versus reality.

- **Assets under Management (AUM) Changes**: AUM growth can be problematic because no strategy is infinitely scalable. At a certain point, a manager is no longer taking advantage of a market inefficiency; instead he basically is the market. At this point, it is foolish to expect past success to continue. Furthermore, as a manager's AUM grows along with his reputation, he may be tempted to focus more on the management fee rather than the incentive fee, which may minimize his ability to generate absolute returns.

On the flip side, a manager may become bored with grinding out attractive absolute and risk-adjusted returns after they have reached a high level of success and/or growth. As a result, he may start to swing for the fences and inevitably strike out. Perhaps that manager has become so rich that he can easily withstand a 50 percent loss, but investors should not be the victim of such hubris and ignorance of prudent risk management practices.

Although this is just a short list of the factors that must be constantly triangulated by successful hedge fund investors, information unto itself does not lead to thoughtful investment decisions. That being said, the more relevant information one has, the better one is able to process that information in a cogent manner, and the more likely one is to make thoughtful investment decisions that manage risk and generate attractive returns.

One last note—not every manager will perform well with every market movement, but what is important is that they are doing what they say they are going to do. It is during monitoring that one must be ruthless. If the manager is off thesis or investment discipline, or his strategy just isn't right for the current market environment, then it's time to don your Donald Trump toupee and announce, "You're fired." It is very important to stay on this. Like gardens, relationships need to be pruned or they can get out of hand.

If all of this sounds way too complicated for you to do on your own, the next chapter will provide you with an alternative investment vehicle that will help you navigate the hedge fund world.

In the Words of a Fund of Hedge Fund Legend . . .

John Burbank, Founder & Chief Investment Officer, Passport Capital

1. How would you define a fund of hedge fund?

     As an investment vehicle: In my view, a hedge fund should be an incentives-aligned risk-seeking vehicle that can encompass virtually any investment strategy under any market condition. As a business: A hedge fund is a fragile yet dynamic business that highly rewards independent thinking, market savvy, emotional fortitude, and the ability to learn and change faster than other market participants.

2. **How or why did you get started in the industry?**

I began investing at business school at Stanford but didn't seek a job in it until I was 30 years old and three years out of school. Having been an entrepreneur previously to enable paying for college and business school, my hypothesis of what I was meant to do changed when I tested the idea that I might more likely be wired to be an investor as opposed to an entrepreneur. After borrowing money and trading for a year I found a job after six months of searching with a five-month-old $2 million AUM Emerging Markets fund that needed research help. Despite working for just $1,000 per month for the first year, the experience of learning about the rest of the world outside the U.S. has proven invaluable in forming my macro views and understanding of world markets thereafter. While based in San Francisco, the experience of witnessing the EM crisis in 1997 to 1998 and resulting tech bubble in 1998 to 1999 helped form my lasting market view that price is a liar and the biggest secular changes are generally both the least understood and cause the most price movement in time.

3. **What hedge fund strategies do you use?**

Global long/short equity with a strong emphasis on macro analysis, fundamental research, and risk management.

4. **What do you see as the future of the industry?**

I believe the alternative investment universe will gradually dominate the investment industry, yet the fragility of the business model, the evolving organizational requirements, and the discovery of best practices under challenging market conditions in this era make it hard to see exactly how things will shake out. However, I believe that hedge funds will collectively outperform all other forms of actively managed strategies and thus I believe that growth and evolution are inevitable for the hedge fund industry. As long as the world saves money it will need to be invested increasingly by the best managers using the most favorable vehicles that can withstand volatility and manage risk.

The Men Behind the Curtains

Fund of Hedge Funds

> *A fund of funds due to the fees involved will, over time, under-perform the ETF on the S&P 500. I'll betcha.*
> —Warren Buffett (well, not really)

OKAY. WARREN BUFFETT NEVER uttered the words above, but he may as well have. In 2008, the Oracle of Omaha bet Protégé Partners LLC—a money management firm that runs a fund of hedge funds—that the returns from a low-cost S&P 500 Index fund sold by Vanguard will out-perform the average returns delivered by 5 fund of hedge funds (net of fees, costs, and expenses) over 10 years.

Having put up roughly $320,000 on each side, this winner-takes-all wager is serious business. Although the 2007 to 2009 economic crisis put Buffett behind, he is now closing the gap. But, the fact remains that many people question the validity of this alternative investment vehicle that provides investors with access to the historically inaccessible world of hedge funds and their legendary managers.

So, what is a fund of hedge funds? As the name implies, it is a fund that invests in other hedge funds. In creating and managing a portfolio of various hedge funds, a fund of hedge funds manager thematically blends together funds so as to maximize returns while minimizing risk. To do so, he must create a diversified portfolio that is composed of funds that exhibit low correlations with the overall market, experience solid performance, and have lower volatility. Thus, funds of hedge funds are the ultimate vehicle for investors who want to take advantage of the various benefits of hedge fund investing.

If done properly, smaller investors—who historically do not have the sizable minimums required to get access to hall of fame hedge fund managers—allot their capital to this alternative asset, with the capital being stewarded judiciously to an able-minded group that is constantly and dynamically shifting the portfolio.

Boy, that was a mouthful! So, let's start learning the ins and outs of these funds of hedge funds.

A Quick History Lesson

The first fund of hedge funds, Leveraged Capital Holdings (LCH), was founded by George Karlweis in Geneva in 1969. Its mandate was simple: Invest in the best hedge fund managers so as to piggyback on the absolute returns they garnered. Witnessing the success of LCH, Grosvenor Partners founded the first U.S. fund of hedge funds just two short years later. Then, in 1973, Jean Perret and Steve Mallory—better known throughout the industry as Permal—launched Haussmann Holdings N.V., which became the leading European multimanager and multi-strategy fund of hedge funds.

Since then, funds of hedge funds have grown substantially, reaching exponential levels of growth in the early to mid 2000s during the hedge fund glory days. The industry attracted many investors who longed to gain access to some of the top hedge fund managers—George Soros, Michael Steinhardt, and Julian Robertson. As these funds had extremely high minimums, the fund of hedge funds model would bundle together smaller orders that would then be invested directly into the funds. Fund of hedge funds version 2.0 came when the industry added the bells and whistles of analytical research and portfolio resource allocation.

Suffice it to say, the industry was crushed during the 2007 to 2009 economic crisis, which was further intensified by the devious acts of fraud of managers like Bernie

Madoff. No wonder there is a tremendous cabal in the investment industry aligned against funds of hedge funds.

Today, there are over 2,018 funds of hedge funds in the world. Many estimates show that close to 22 percent of all new investments into hedge funds are coming from funds of hedge funds. Since their advent, funds of hedge funds have been the vehicle of choice for new entrants into the hedge fund space. As a result, they manage approximately 32 percent of the hedge fund industry with approximately $639 billion under management as of September 30, 2011.

This growth rate may be attributed to their overall performance. As their mandate is to build long-term compounding capital, their objective is to achieve stable and consistent returns. Table 9.1 shows the annual returns of funds of hedge funds compared to the S&P from 2006 to 2011.

Table 9.1   Comparable Performance: HFRI Fund of Funds vs. S&P 500 TR

	S&P 500 TR	HFRI Fund of Funds
2006	15.79%	10.39%
2007	5.49%	10.25%
2008	−36.99%	−21.37%
2009	26.47%	11.47%
2010	15.07%	5.70%
2011	2.12%	−5.56%
Standard Deviation (2006–2011)	17.41%	6.50%

Source: Data provided by PerTrac, Hedge Fund Research, Inc.

More than Just a Middleman

Remember the Dream Team. You know, the 1992 men's Olympic basketball team that featured active NBA players like Michael Jordan, Scottie Pippen, Magic Johnson, David Robinson . . . I could go on and on—who dominated the world of basketball. No longer made up of inexperienced college players, this hand-picked team went on to win the gold medal in Barcelona, have their charactures affixed to T-shirts worn nationwide, and become known as the strongest team ever assembled in the history of any sport. A fund of hedge funds manager seeks to create a similar type of Dream Team. Imagine the lineup now—from SAC Capital, with a 5 percent allocation, Steven A. Cohen; from Third Point Management, with a 4.5 percent allocation, Daniel Loeb; and so on. Before you know it you step back and you have a skillful group of managers with proven track records. What's more, their investment disciplines blend together in such a way that they perfectly complement your portfolio. Like the conductor of an orchestra, the fund of hedge funds manager meticulously selects each musician with an eye and ear to how they fit together to produce Carnegie Hall–worthy music.

In the mid 2000s, the fund of hedge funds industry had amassed over $400 billion in assets under management. In nimbly shifting capital among different hedge fund managers and strategies, these investing vehicles were envied by hedge funds managers who zealously sought to cut out the middleman by setting up multistrategy funds. And, yet, funds of funds hung tough, accounting for over 40 percent of all new investments into hedge funds during that time period. The main reason why many funds of hedge funds outperformed multistrategy funds is related to choice. Funds of hedge funds can choose from the best of the best; without the dilemma of having an in-house manager by their side, they can be more ruthless.[1]

Similar to a hedge fund, a fund of hedge funds is run by a managing partner who oversees all of the investing decisions. Typically, they are organized as a limited partnership or limited liability corporation, which transfers unlimited liability to the managing partner and restricted liability for limited partners who assume risk up to the level of their investment only.

Essentially, a fund of hedge funds is *one* investor in a hedge fund who acts on behalf of *multiple* investors who allocate capital to their fund of hedge funds. This collected pool of capital—assets under management—enables them to meet the investing threshold of certain hedge funds that have a high level of entry.

Unlike a hedge fund, the fund of hedge funds manager does *not* make direct investments in securities himself.

Instead, he invests in a multiple number of actual hedge funds so as to enhance diversification. This blending of different funds—that exhibit different investing strategies and represent multiple asset classes—delivers a more consistent return than any individual fund because it lowers the total risk of the portfolio. As such, a fund of hedge funds' emphasis is on long-term performance with minimal volatility.

So, just how does a fund of hedge funds manager allocate his portfolio?

In order to employ a repeatable investment process that achieves risk-adjusted returns and protects capital, the portfolio manager conducts forward-looking fundamental research that focuses on the evolution of opportunity sets and the ability of the manager to execute a given strategy. In other words, the fund of funds manager slices and dices hedge funds—choosing the best and the brightest—so that he can customize the right asset allocation mix to hit a total return target.

Then, he constructs a portfolio that thematically and tactically allocates assets among more than 20 hedge fund managers and strategies that are better able to account for global macroeconomic conditions and specific opportunities. In doing so, he focuses on selecting a series of non-correlated (or low) funds so as to diversify risk exposures. In other words, he targets and selects hedge funds that are fundamentally different from one another. This diversification can be achieved by investing in different asset classes, sectors, or geographic regions. In doing so, he enhances the returns of the portfolio while reducing risk.

Along the way, he adds additional value by actively shifting investment exposure to emerging opportunity sets with an attractive risk/reward proposition and correlation characteristics. After all, the world and the investing world are constantly changing. As such, he needs to make sure that the portfolio can be quickly adjusted to the changing global economic realities.

Ultimately, the overall performance of a fund of hedge funds is a function of this strategic portfolio construction that is based on hedge fund strategy outlook, hedge fund manager selection, and liquidity and risk management. If done appropriately, this allocation will minimize volatility and maximize risk returns.

The Specifics

The best and brightest in the fund of funds industry do the following three things for their clients:

1. They have a deep understanding of the macroeconomic situations and the global economy, taking into account what the Federal Reserve and other central banks are doing and also what is going on

in the world's currency and commodities markets. This insight goes deep. It could be talking to Fed officials and the world's brightest economists and former and current policy makers. It could also include a decent understanding of the geopolitical situation and an internal heat map of where all of the major risks are on the globe.

2. Based on this assessment, the portfolio team will then develop a model of the right mix of hedge fund strategies to coincide with what is going on globally. This will be the model portfolio and it will change dynamically. The group will be keen to make these changes as circumstances themselves change.

3. After working on the macroeconomic picture and the relevant themes it is the job of the portfolio research team to cull through each strategy in an effort to pick the best funds in each category. There might be 1,200 funds out of 9,000 that are rigorously reviewed and researched. These funds are rated on things like track record, potential style drift, continuity of management, and personnel (with the key people being subjected to a private investigatory search). There will then be a full operational review of the company and its vendors including its prime broker, accountants,

lawyers, and so on. This process is rigorous and disciplined and there are no shortcuts taken. Anything that sounds too good to be true is deemed such and kicked immediately into the waste bucket. There is also an emphasis on finding people who know how to create the right culture and value system for their staff.

After this process is complete, the job of the fund of funds manager is to let the hedge funds be hedge funds. Step back and let the managers do their jobs pursuant to their respective disciplines.

Your Dream Team

In order to provide investors with these risk-adjusted returns, a fund of hedge funds must employ a management team that has the skills required to identify the appropriate hedge funds that provide such diversification while reducing risk. These professionals must possess knowledge of the most complex financial instruments and investing strategies and have the ability to identify and understand risk characteristics. These skills will enable them to better conduct the fundamental, quantitative, and qualitative investment analysis needed to assess the potential drawdowns for each manager in each strategy so that they may determine the appropriate asset mix.

A fund of hedge funds must also assemble a high-caliber operational due diligence team that fully assesses the hedge fund manager and portfolio. As discussed in Chapter 8, this team must thematically evaluate the hedge fund manager's strategy, experience, assets, operations, and pedigree.

How do funds of hedge funds accumulate this collection? This is the job of the sales and marketing team. Like any product, the fund needs to be categorized and then segmented from a marketing perspective. It is the job of the sales team to then go out and identify prospects who have a demand for hedge fund investing but do not want to go directly to the manager due to lack of size or possibly expertise. Some managers might be on the distribution platforms of some of the retail wire houses. If that's true, it is likely that they have gone through a rigorous due diligence by that institution before a financial consultant can suggest the fund as part of the overall product offering of the firm.

In the end, fund of funds managers garner assets the old-fashioned way: lots of meetings, tons of presentations—maybe with some bagels and coffee and doughnuts thrown in—but ultimately they have to have a product that does what they say it does, and then the sales team will have no problem accruing assets under management and advisory.

The Pluses . . .

As discussed throughout this *Little Book*, investors are often intimidated by the mysterious and opaque world of hedge funds. Given this inherent level of diminished transparency of hedge funds, funds of hedge funds provide investors with the resources and tools needed to efficiently access the alternative investment arena so that they may make investment decisions in an efficient, thoughtful, and timely manner. As discussed in the previous section, there are various benefits to investing in a fund of hedge funds. They include the following.

Access

Do you have $10 million? I didn't think so . . . not many people do—not even many institutions do. Yet, that astronomical number is sometimes the minimum amount required to invest with some of the world's finest hedge fund managers. Funds of hedge funds solve this problem.

Funds of hedge funds are an investing vehicle that provides access to unrepresented investors who historically were unable to enter this space because of their limited capital and/or capital restrictions imposed by hedge funds. Given the high investment requirements of certain hedge funds, a fund of hedge funds provides investors with the ability to invest in hedge funds that they normally would not be able to access. Moreover, they expose investors to a broader array of hedge fund investing styles, strategies, and managers.

A quick note: As discussed in Chapter 1, hedge funds may only provide access to *accredited* investors. Again, accredited investors are individuals who have a minimum of $1 million in net worth, excluding the value of their primary residence, and entities that have a minimum of $5 million in total assets.

Specifically, certain funds of funds—such as SkyBridge Capital—offer products that provide high-net-worth individuals and mid-sized institutions with the opportunity to invest in this space. For example, for as little as $50,000 a Registered Investment Company (RIC) provides individuals with access through the same aggregation that a fund of funds provides. These types of products put relatively small investors in the catbird seat, benefitting from the aggregation but also from the rigorous analysis and risk management.

Diversification = Mitigated Risk

As discussed previously, a fund of hedge funds holds a diversified portfolio of various hedge funds that invest in different asset classes, alternative investment styles, and geographic regions. Although there is not a magic number, it is recommended that a fund of hedge funds invest in about 30 to 50 managers, with the typical sweet spot being around 35 to 40 managers.

In composing a portfolio of multiple hedge funds, a fund of hedge funds diversifies holdings, which, in turn, diversifies idiosyncratic risks. Specifically, its model helps mitigate the risk of directly investing in hedge funds because it diversifies risk thematically by multiple asset class exposure. In doing so, it reduces the risk associated with investing in a single hedge fund or hedge fund manager. This provides a safeguard to the portfolio to ensure that no single blowup with any hedge fund will severely affect the portfolio.

Professional and Timely Monitoring

After reading the rather overwhelming and extensive due diligence questionnaire mentioned in the previous chapter and available in the appendix, it's no wonder why many investors shy away from investing in hedge funds, preferring to allocate their hard-earned dollars to easier-to-understand stock and bond investing. Funds of hedge funds solve this problem by employing managers who:

- Conduct due diligence on the manager and his portfolio selection.
- Thematically allocate the investors' capital among various asset classes and strategies.

- Constantly monitor the hedge fund's manager, portfolio allocation, and performance.

In doing so, they alleviate the burden from the investor who may not have ample time, resources, or skills to adequately do so.

. . . and the Minuses

That being said, there are also a few disadvantages associated with investing in this space, including the following.

Fees

Typically, funds of hedge funds charge an extra layer of fees *on top of* the fees already imposed by the hedge fund. As discussed throughout this *Little Book*, the hedge fund manager is already charging a performance + an incentive fee; the fund of hedge funds adds an additional 1 to 2 percent. That's a whole lot of fees!

Why is it so expensive? Well, in life you often get what you pay for—and you often have to pay for service. Think about it: A person who invests in a fund of hedge funds is essentially hiring a chief investment officer to allocate his assets across a broad spectrum of managers. This requires time, energy, effort, and due diligence. Now, imagine if that same investor had to set up an investment office to do this sort of work—the expense would be astronomical . . . not to mention, he would never be able to access some of the greatest hedge fund minds that the fund of hedge funds manager can access. Nor, would he have the expertise to conduct the necessary research and analysis needed to add meaningful value to the portfolio. Just like many corporations outsource their payroll departments or use databases that are part of the cloud, investors should think of a fund of hedge funds as cloud investing or outsourced investing.

But let's be honest—there will always be people who think funds of hedge funds are too costly and not worth their hard-earned dollars. In fact, we started this chapter with one of the richest men in America saying that they aren't! He might be right, but then again he may be wrong. After all, at the time of this writing, Protégé Partners is ahead of the Oracle from Omaha. It may end badly for the fund of funds folks on this bet, but one thing is irrefutable—funds of hedge funds just flat out perform better in down markets.

Madoff Factor

Bernard L. Madoff Investment Securities LLC wasn't a hedge fund or a fund of hedge funds. Madoff was a broker-dealer who did more damage to the hedge fund industry than any actual manager in history—even more damage than the now-defunct *Trader Monthly* magazine!

Year in and year out, he would grind out consistent and low double-digit returns so as not to drawn attention to his devious plan and keep his clients happy. What's more, he offered allegedly liquid investments where people could get their money out monthly. (There was deception in the liquidity and as long as he was able to find future willing investors he could keep the game going in perpetuity.) And yet, he was never able to offer any transparency as to his investment process, philosophy, or allocation. Interesting.

Fund of fund managers (some of them at least) took the easy way out and allocated aggressively to Madoff. And so, several funds of hedge funds—Fairfield Greenwich and Tremont Partners, to name two—took the easy way out and allocated aggressively to Mr. Madoff and his fraudulent Ponzi scheme. That is disgraceful! What happened to all of the research and risk management and due diligence? Any cursory review of Madoff would have caused a shunning of Madoff, as if he were a leper in a nudist colony! After all, he was self–taught and had an unknown accountant who worked out of a storefront across the Tappan Zee Bridge. How could they invest with such a manager?

The Madoff Factor gave the industry a bad rap and set it back big time . . . and almost completely shut it down in Europe. As the expression goes—a few bad apples can spoil the entire barrel. The same can be said about the fund of hedge funds industry. Just ask politicians, gun-toting rap singers, mortgage brokers, investment bankers, and a whole host of others!

As a result of these few sour apples, the image of the fund of hedge funds industry was tarnished. Who needs to pay the additional fees if the fund of hedge funds managers aren't properly researching the managers they ultimately give the money to? (The irony was that Madoff wasn't even running a hedge fund or a fund of hedge funds; he was running a separate account business that made tons of money, and thousands of clients bucketed him in the world of alternatives. Regulation never stopped Madoff . . . the recession exposed him.) And yet, what the newspapers neglect to mention are the funds of hedge funds that are performing and abiding by the law. There aren't a lot of stories written about them—that's boring. Disasters, crashes, thievery—that's exciting!

And so, an investor needs to do a little more home-work before investing with *anyone* . . .

How to Avoid the Next Madoff

Madoff's cover was simple—"I need to keep my secret sauce and alchemy from being exposed to the big accountants and prime brokers." People, listen up, come closer to the book: *There is no secret sauce!* Not now, not ever.

Of course, I couldn't end this chapter on such a sour note. I wouldn't be doing my job as your sage if I didn't provide you with five tips for avoiding the next Bernie.

1. **Do Your Due Diligence**: Although we discussed this at length in the previous chapter, managers must explain their investing process and portfolio strategy. An investor must take the time to visit the manager's office and conduct proper on-site operational due diligence. If the manager refuses this request, don't even think about investing with him.

2. **Get to Know the Manager's Service Providers**: Make sure your manager is using one of the biggest, most well-known prime brokers as well as a recognizable, reputable accounting firm for auditing the books and records of the fund.

3. **Follow the Money**: Investors must be aware of who touches the money and where it goes. Having a globally known administrator in the mix will further ease anxiety and add another layer of protection.

4. **No Backie, No Shirtie**: Okay, that wasn't that funny. But never allocate money unless the manager agrees to subject him or herself to a background check. Don't write the ticket without it.

5. **Smell the Air**: Use your gut; sometimes you just know when something isn't right. Follow your instincts. There are many hedge fund managers in the sea. It is always okay to pass on the one you question.

Okay. Enough with this negativity. Let's find out how to score a job—or your kid a job—at the next hedge fund powerhouse!

In the Words of a Fund of Hedge Fund Legend . . .

Ray Nolte, Managing Partner, SkyBridge Capital

1. **How would you define a fund of hedge fund?**

   In its simplest form a hedge fund of funds, "FOF" is best defined as a collection of individual hedge funds combined within a single fund structure. In reality a hedge fund of funds can take on numerous forms and may be comprised of a limited number or a significant large number of underlying funds. While the FOF may be constructed to focus on a single hedge fund strategy utilizing multiple managers it may also be comprised of multiple managers focused on many of the different hedge fund strategies. The investment object of an FOF can also vary significantly in terms of its volatility, return objective, and it's correlation to various other asset classes.

2. **How or why did you get started in the industry?**

My career began in the capital markets focused on sales and trading across currencies, interest rates, equities, and later derivatives. From that I migrated to structured investment products and then to CIO of an asset management business focused on globally diversified portfolios of stocks, bonds, and cash. Around that same time hedge funds were starting to become recognized investment alternatives with attractive risk adjusted returns and correlation characteristics. Therefore, I began to explore how to utilize them within a portfolio of traditional asset classes to create portfolios that would be more efficient. As a result I concluded that a multi manager multi-strategy fund of funds would be the best solution to achieve the desired object of migrating a traditional portfolio toward the northwest quadrant of the efficient frontier.

3. **What hedge fund strategies do you use?**

The short answer is: I believe one should be as unconstrained as possible when building portfolios. Therefore I would consider investing in just about any strategy. That said strategies that utilize significant leverage or primarily invest in illiquid securities or are short volatility should generally be avoided. There are times in a market cycle that these strategies may be desirable to be included in a portfolio but allocations should generally be smaller than many of the other strategies.

4. **What do you see as the future of the industry?**

I believe the hedge fund industry will continue to grow and fund of funds will remain a significant part of the industry's growth. Fund of funds will continue to provide managers due diligence and strategy selection to those investors that do not have the resources or wherewithal to perform these activities on their own. I believe the industry will bifurcate with some funds gravitating toward those that can be better characterized as hedge fund beta providers while others will be better thought of as alpha providers. I anticipate that the beta orientated manager will experience fee compression as a result of delivering less value to their investors. In effect these managers will be similar to indexed long only funds. Other FOFs will take on a more active roll in building their portfolios by taking on specific sector or manager exposures. These managers will be better classified as alpha managers and to the extent they deliver superior returns will be able to charge higher fees for delivering a more attractive return stream to their clients. Additionally I believe that as the industry grows there will be a gradual blurring between traditional active managers and hedge fund managers. In the end I believe that hedge funds and FOFs, which are simply portfolios of underlying hedge funds, do not really represent anything other than a more robust way to create return streams that are complementary to traditional client portfolios.

Chapter Ten

From Wall Street to Park Avenue

Setting Up Shop at the Hedge Fund Hotel

No other career in finance gives you the freedom to be your own boss and invest in anything, anywhere, that gets your juices flowing. . . . And most important: Nowhere else on Wall Street can you get so rich, so fast, so young.
—Bethany McLean, "Everybody's Going Hedge Funds," *Fortune*, June 8, 1998

PRIOR TO THE ECONOMIC crisis of 2007 to 2009, the best and brightest were lured to Park Avenue and Greenwich, Connecticut, in the hopes of scoring a job at a prominent hedge fund or, better yet, starting their own fund! Intrigued by the exclusive world of hedge funds, these young hopefuls had visions of dollar signs, private jets, and beautiful women dancing in their heads. Who can blame them? Everywhere you turned, it seemed that there was another article glorifying a hedge fund super-hero who was making millions of millions of dollars in just one year! (And by millions, I mean three-figure millions! In 2005, it was reported that the top 25 hedge fund managers were making an average of $363 million a year!) Article after article prophesied the hedge fund invasion of Wall Street, claiming: "Today, the money that talks the loudest in America belongs to a closely knit, inscrutable group of men who run hedge funds."

Although those days of economic windfall may have passed, the mysterious world of hedge funds still attracts many of the so-called best and the brightest, causing many a manager of mutual funds to worry about who will manage the "big money" in the future. While it is out of the scope of this *Little Book*—and perhaps a book onto itself—to explore the answer to that seemingly complicated question, I am more interested in helping readers, especially those in college or graduate school, get a job in the industry.

If you are a college or graduate student who is interested in securing a job at a hedge fund, or are a parent of a young, ambitious, Alex P. Keaton–like child who wants to dispense advice to his or her child on how to access this mysterious arena, then this is the chapter for you. In it, we'll discuss:

- The migration of hedge fund talent from the world of investment banking to the hedge fund industry.
- How to get a job at a top hedge fund.

But, this chapter will also be a cautionary tale. If you are looking to chase money, fortune, or fame and don't think you have the stomach for managing money or being a part of an asset management organization, then hopefully you will go back to your art or poetry class when you are done reading this chapter. As I tell any young person I advise or mentor: follow your passions and do want you really want to do. Don't chase what you think you should do; it will only delay your journey to job and life fulfillment.

Wall Street's Mass Migration

Growing up, it was fairly simple. Whenever I was asked what I wanted to be when I grew up, my answer was always the same: I wanted a job that would give me and my family financial security. At the time, I had no idea what a hedge fund was and if someone asked me I probably would have said it had to do with landscaping (as in hedges) and nothing to do with money management.

When I graduated college and law school in the 1980s, the dream job was to work in investment banking. At the time, newspapers, magazines, and journalists glorified the lavish lifestyles of investment bankers and corporate raiders. As hedge fund managers weren't yet on the media's radar screen, it wasn't in the consciousness of the undergraduate wannabe financier. So, the yuppie puppies at Harvard, including me, all signed up for the biggest, lowest-risk firms that we thought could offer the highest reward and paycheck. Goldman Sachs was the most effective of all the firms at recruiting the best and the brightest, so naturally I set my eyes on the prize. In 1989, I was hired as an associate in the investment banking division of the firm and was on my way to a lifestyle of champagne wishes and caviar dreams . . . that was, until I got fired less than two years into the job. The truth was, I wasn't a fit for the world of investment banking. My knowledge base, skill set, and personality were better suited for a position on the firm's sales team and eventually private wealth management. I was even better suited for the world of entrepreneurship and money management . . . but we'll get to that in a minute.

Unlike when I started my career, the days of wanting to pursue investment banking per se are over. In the late 1990s, it seemed that everyone wanted to work at a hedge fund or start their own fund. From seasoned money managers to up-and-coming MBAs to college students working out of their dorms, everywhere you turned some whiz kid (and in some cases, some not so whiz kid) was starting his own fund.

During that time, I, too, caught the hedge fund fever. Seven years out of law school I began my journey and entered the industry by cofounding Oscar Capital with Andrew K. Boszhardt Jr.

So, what was the cause of this mass migration?

- **Earnings Potential:** Just as insects are attracted to light, money managers are attracted to lucrative fee structures. Take that and throw in the fact that the money manager is joining an exclusive secret club and it's easy to see why the industry boomed. In the last decade, the top hedge fund managers earned "more money than God in a couple of years of trading," amassing more wealth than the mightiest masters of the universe at prominent investment banks and private equity firms. As Sebastian Mallaby says in his insightful book, *More Money than God,* "In 2006, Goldman Sachs awarded its chief executive, Lloyd C. Blankfien, an unprecedented $54 million, but the *bottom guy* on *Alpha* magazine's list of the top 25 hedge fund earners reportedly took home $240 million . . . [and] the top three hedge-fund moguls each were said to have earned more than $1 billion."

Using A.W. Jones, infamous fee structure, hedge fund managers have huge earning potential. As one former hedge fund manager said, "It's the best way for an able money manager to accumulate really serious money quickly. It is better than being a rock star or a professional athlete."[1]

But, as the 2007 to 2009 economic crisis proved, hedge funds can also be an abominable way to lose money and the odds of super success are quite limited. As many hedge fund failures have shown us, hedge fund managers have put in time and great expense only to experience their shop being shut down as a result of market forces, poor performance, and a lack of interest.

- **No Dead Weight**: The ability to use a broad selection of alternative investing strategies and tools to make money while controlling your risk in any market is also very appealing to the aspiring money manager. Unlike a vanilla mutual fund portfolio, hedge funds grant managers a license to invest in a plethora of asset classes using various investing strategies and a seemingly endless stream of financial tools.

- **Entrepreneuralism**: Ah . . . the freedom to be
  your own boss and run your own shop. Make your
  own rules. Cut loose from the restraints of a large,
  bureaucratic organization. Actively manage your
  clients' money. Live and die by your own performance. These are the sentiments felt by aspiring
  money managers all around the country. This is
  what drove Andrew Boszhardt and I back in 1996.
  We wanted to see if we could be successful on our
  own without the incredible brand name of Goldman
  Sachs behind us. We had our ups and downs and
  nothing can mature you faster than being out on
  your own fending for yourself. As Andrew used to
  say, "If you don't break away from your parents,
  you can never claim 100 percent."

- **Infrastructure**: Unlike a mutual fund's complex
  administrative infrastructure, a hedge fund has a
  relatively small start-up process. In 1998, it was
  estimated that a manager simply needed $15,000
  to $50,000 to cover legal fees, accounting costs,
  supplies, and overhead. And one 2005 article
  quoted a hedge fund manager as saying, "To run
  money, which is how managers refer to what they
  do, requires little more than a few computers."[2]
  That number has significantly increased over
  the years—it is more like $125,000 today—but the

fact remains that there is relatively little overhead required to set up a fund . . . obviously, this statement doesn't account for the amount of money a managing partner actually puts into the fund himself. That being said, here's my blunt advice to anyone who is thinking of starting a fund—*don't do it!*

Okay, okay. So, I might sound like a hypocrite with my advice here. After all, I started my own fund. But the truth of the matter is that I didn't set out on that path—it just happened. My advice? Pay your dues. Start by first getting a job at a hedge fund; learn the business from the inside out, and then see if you are still interested in running your own shop. Perhaps after you read the stories below, you'll realize you no longer have the stomach for this business.

Only the Strongest Survive

Working at a hedge fund is not an easy task. Many firms have a zero-tolerance attitude with a reputation for high turnover where only the strongest of managers survive. Ken Griffin, legendary manager of Citadel LLC, has been known to compare the hedge fund job market to buses where people get on, people get off, and the bus keeps rolling forward. He says, "People say 'it's a tough place to work. It's demanding. Its unrelenting.' I look at these as strengths inherent in strong companies. . . . I'm very proud that we have a sterling reputation when it comes to doing what we say we're going to do." Amen to that.

There is a passionate pursuit of excellence in shops like Citadel, and there really isn't a lot of room for lazy crybabies. The new generation who received trophies for every soccer game and ninth place track finishes better be prepared. There is no room for whining or entitlement. A willing attitude is everything—it is for those who have no issue with menial work. For those who don't think that hard tasks that may not be instantly gratifying are beneath them. People who exhibit these qualities will fit in and thrive. So, you better cowboy up. Do grunt work with a smile, and be willing to do more than whatever it states on your lifeless job description.

If this advice doesn't make you weak in the knees, try working for someone like Michael Steinhardt, one of Wall Street's most successful hedge fund managers, who notoriously had red-faced tirades where he yelled unmercifully at his staff. According to his best-selling book, he even went as far as to chastise an employee who suggesting killing himself after mismanaging some bonds. "All I want to do is kill myself," he said. To which Steinhardt replied, "Can I watch?"[3] Ouch! You're laughing (or at least smirking right now), but if this were happening to you a week before bonuses, would you cry? Would you? If so, run—don't walk—to another profession.

Inside the Mind of a Super Capitalist

As Mallaby so keenly reports, "Hedge funds are vehicles for loners and contrarians, for individualists whose ambitions are too big to fit into established financial institutions." They aren't the corporate obsequious types. And yet, hedge fund managers come in many different shapes and sizes—from PhDs in quantitative finance (Cliff Asness of AQR Capital Management) to college students trading convertible bonds out of their Ivy League dorm rooms (Ken Griffin of Citadel) to nerdy, mathematical quants (James Simons of Renaissance Technologies) to hyper, passionate, active traders (Daniel Loeb of Third Point).

As it would be impossible to define the true essence of a hedge fund manager, below are some interesting—and somewhat humorous—insights into the psychographic portraits of these masters of the universe. According to a survey conducted by Russ Alan Prince, author of *Fortune Fortress*:

- **Money Talks**: 89.8 percent of hedge fund professionals view the hedge fund business as the way to become rich.
- **Ego Personified**: 97 percent of hedge fund managers see their portfolios as themselves personified.
- **A Sausage Party**: 92.2 percent of hedge fund managers are men.

- **Icarus Complex**: 54 percent of hedge fund managers say they constantly think about failure. On the other hand, 46 percent think that they will succeed. Perhaps there is an egocentric complex in the works.

- **Free Market Persuasion**: 60.5 percent of hedge fund managers are registered Republicans, while 28.6 percent are registered Democrats. It's no wonder that many hedge fund managers believe in free markets and are fiscally conservative.

- **It's Just Not True**: 33 percent of people surveyed think that the average hedge fund manager makes more than $10 million a year.

While the list above was somewhat provided to be more entertaining than informative, the fact of the matter is that all hedge fund managers share a few traits in common; they are all motivated individuals who have tremendous ambitions that contribute to both their successes and failures; they have a commonality of confidence and a work ethic that drives them and makes them succeed while not taking success for granted.

So, what does it take to land a job in the world of hedge funds . . . or simply land your dream job? A few years ago, a friend of mine asked me that very same question. Here's the list of attributes and skills that I have learned from life and business experience that the next generation of entrepreneurs should have:

- Be confident in yourself as early in your career as possible.
- Prepare for—and always expect—the unexpected.
- Think about the life you want to lead and then determine the steps you need to take to get there.
- Take risks; don't let your fear of failure stop you.
- Don't let failures or setbacks derail your confidence.
- Always look for new opportunities for learning.

If you come at the game from this perspective, you will always be a winner regardless of the outcome.

A Quick Pop Quiz

Before I dispense advice on how to get a job at a hedge fund, I urge you to think long and hard about whether your personality is suited for this high-paced, intense, live-or-die-by-your-own-performance lifestyle. Take this quick pop quiz to find out:

1. Is my personality suited for a high-pressure, risk-taking culture?
2. Do I have the ability to quickly and efficiently analyze and synthesize data and information?

3. Am I able to handle rejection?

4. If something has gone wrong, can I acknowledge it and cut my losses quickly?

5. Do I have a sense of humor? That's right—a sense of humor. Come on, where do you think all of those trading desk jokes come from—someone has to think them up!

6. The market is down. My firm is faced with redemptions. Can I ride high in the saddle and think rationally about the future without allowing my emotions to derail me or the firm?

7. Am I able to realize that some of my portfolio moves are outside of my control and are due to exogenous events, while others are a result of my expertise? Can I separate the two? And, when things go wrong, can I remain objective about the world and any contribution that I have made to the portfolio?

8. Can I build up the other members of my team? Can I share in the successes and failures of my team? Can I make sure not to hoard ideas or take credit for other people's ideas? Can I be someone whom other teammates look up to and want to work alongside?

9. Will I commit myself to constant improvement—either by reading, going to conferences, continuing

my education, traveling, or meeting with other analysts and portfolio managers? Will I be a constant source of new knowledge and innovation?

10. Will I be a person who is a symbol of all things positive about the firm? Will I help the firm recruit a diversity of new and exciting talent and help to mentor them when they arrive?

If you answered "yes," to all these questions, then you will have maximized your position and your ability to get a job in this industry—or any industry!

Okay, I am off my pedantic know-it-all soapbox. Let's get down to the facts and the suggestions that will help you find a job.

Scoring a Job at a Hedge Fund

How will you know that the hedge fund industry is for you? No rock is going to hit you from the sky; no high priestess is going to paint your forehead. You will just know. It will burn in your gut. It will make you want to read everything that has been written about the industry. You will feel excited around analysis and using your wits against others in a broad, vast, and competitive market. You will want to over-question everyone that is in the industry. You will lay awake at night thinking about game theory and risk management scenarios. And lastly, you will never ever give up your job search no matter how daunting it appears to break into the industry.

So, if you are looking for a job at a hedge fund, you are in luck! According to recent surveys, hedge fund job listings increased by 32 percent in 2010. Unfortunately, there isn't a scientific recipe that I can give you to help you land a job at the next hedge fund powerhouse. But, below are some suggestions on how to score an interview.

- **The Blind Outreach Program**: The blind outreach program occurs when you hit the mail merge on your computer and e-mail your resume to all of the personnel departments in the hedge fund universe. Although this may be the coldest of cold calls—and probably the least effective approach—I still think it is necessary as it forces you to get your arms around the many different names in the industry. After all, you have to first compile the database and do your homework on each fund before you decide you want to send a particular fund this e-mail.

- **Warm Call:** On the other end of the spectrum, the warm call occurs when a friend (of a friend, of a friend, of a friend) gives you an assist by giving you the personal e-mail address and phone number of a person on the inside. Using your network to help you land an interview is always a good idea—there is nothing shameful about asking someone to do you a favor. Although this approach is way more effective than the Blind Outreach Program, it still has its pitfalls and may not result in a direct interview.

- **The Referral**: This is the big one. The referral occurs when a hedge fund manager who is looking to fill a spot reaches out to his network of colleagues and friends looking for someone and your name surfaces.

Once you score an interview, you better be prepared. Being prepared means chasing down and reading every article a Google search turns up about the company and its founders. It means suggesting new investment ideas. It means dressing right and having the right body language. It means asking serious questions. Talk about yourself with candor, nothing canned.

The most successful interview candidates who pass muster with me have three things in common:

1. **Attitude**: "In this economy, I feel lucky to have been given this potential job opportunity."

2. **Philosophy**: "I think like an owner or partner in the firm. I am willing to offer suggestions on how to help the firm grow and will add another dimension of positive team orientation to your culture."

3. **Message**: "I want my career to be at your firm. I have what it takes to add value to your processes while being an important culture carrier to your organization."

Reread these bullets a few times. Think about them. Execute passion, purpose, and conviction. This will undoubtedly increase your odds of landing the position that you covet.

A Final Few Words: 15 Things I Would Do If I Were You

And, now that you got the job, a few more words of advice:

1. **Watch the company that you keep**. If you want to be successful, you have to hang out with successful people. Build your network around fun-loving but industrious people who are full of passion, purpose, and ethics.

2. **Set goals**. Devise a clear plan with measurable objectives and then go after them!

3. **Read—devour everything**. In addition to business magazines like *Forbes*, *Fortune*, and *Bloomberg Businessweek*, make sure you read *Barron's Weekly*, the *Wall Street Journal*, and the *New York Times* daily. The information you read will prepare you for what is going on in the real world. I am not talking cover to cover but a good cursory review of these publications.

4. **Attend seminars and conferences**. Do not pass up networking opportunities particularly at the early stage of your career. Make sure that you trade business cards with as many of your contemporaries as possible.

5. **Share information**. E-mail people in your network interesting things that you have read or seen that you think are worthwhile. Soon, many of those people will be doing the same thing for you, and you will have created a whole new learning and networking tool.

6. **Follow the crowd**. Try to meet people who have the job that you want. Want to be a CFO at a hedge fund? Figure out a way to meet various CFOs. In the age of social media, start following

them on their digital platforms and engage in conversation with them.

7. **Be flexible**. As the world around us is constantly evolving, you must always be ready to adapt to changing circumstances.

8. **Keep a positive file**. This business is nasty and at times downright cruel. When you are brought to your knees by the market or other industry forces, have a file in your desk of fun sayings or inspirational quotes. Maybe included in that file is a nice note from somebody you admire. Or maybe it's a birthday card handmade by your life partner. When things are going badly, break out the file—it will force insight and perspective.

9. **Be grateful**. Over the course of my career, I have found that the happiest and most successful people are those who view themselves as lucky in life. These people are always thankful and optimistic—no matter what their lot in life might be. If you have charity in your bones, that will also make you happy.

10. **Lend a helping hand**. Make sure you do nonlinear nice things for people—with no quid pro quo expected.

11. **Pick a charitable cause**. Pay it forward. Pick a charitable cause that you believe in and that will help humanity. Trust in karma and watch how good things start happening in your career.

12. **Find a mentor**. Set up lunches with the people that you think are important for you to meet. It can't hurt to try. There is nothing more flattering than when someone says they would like to be mentored by you. If you are rebuffed, be polite and figure out ways to start a new mentor relationship.

13. **Ask for favors**. Don't be afraid to ask for a favor. It shows confidence and self-esteem. And you never know, the more times you ask the higher the likelihood that you will eventually get what you want.

14. **Don't compare**. Comparing yourself and your career to your college roommate or city friends will not make you happy.

15. **Be humble**. Hubris and greed have been the cause of many a corporate death. Don't fall victim to these cancerous weapons.

To all of you out there that want it, it can be done. Be optimistic and perseverant in your pursuit.

In the Words of a
Hedge Fund Legend . . .

Daniel S. Loeb, Founder, Third Point

1. **How would you define a hedge fund?**

   So many types of hedge funds have developed since the first AW Jones long/short equity model that today, the only unifying element across the industry is the management and incentive fee compensation structure. A fund should deliver higher absolute returns relative to volatility than the market to earn these fees.

2. **How or why did you get started in the industry?**

   I was passionate about entrepreneurship and the markets from a very young age. By my early 30s, I believed I had acquired sufficient experience investing in diverse strategies across various asset classes to start my own fund. While I was well prepared to begin managing money, I underestimated the importance of having a deep background in business management and leadership, which I have learned on the job. Studying and applying principled business processes is as important as honing your investment skills if your goal is to scale a hedge fund successfully.

3. **What hedge fund strategies do you use?**

   Multistrategy with a focus on event-driven special situations.

4. **What do you see as the future of the industry?**

   Firms with great leadership, high quality teams, thoughtful idea generation processes, and well-articulated investment frameworks will continue to grow. While it is increasingly difficult to start funds, passionate investors with entrepreneurial acumen will persevere and thrive.

Conclusion

The Shape of
Things to Come

~

The obvious isn't obvious until it's obvious.
> —Should have come from Yogi Berra
> but it is really from Anthony Scaramucci

THE HEDGE FUND INDUSTRY doesn't climb a wall of worry;
it climbs a wall of resentment and scorn. For two decades
now, people have sought to demystify the mysterious
nature of hedge funds. They have asserted that the business does not add any value, awards extreme risk takers,

charges ostentatiously high fees, and renders the market unsettled and unstable. Moreover, the media has driven into the skulls of all civilians that hedge funds are baaaad— just plain all baaaaad. Yet there are the true believers— not just the managers themselves and their employees—but also private investors, institutional investors, academics, consultants, and investment officers who beg to differ. It is through a review of hedge fund performance results that they have decided that the industry has merit and value. The obvious is in fact obvious—while there are funds that don't add value, the industry on the whole does, and will continue to grow as a result.

In a recently published book entitled *The Hedge Fund Mirage*, my contemporary and professional colleague, Simon Lack, asserts that the industry is a value trap. Based on his experiences and the numerous examples that he provides in the book, Simon argues that there are very few managers who can generate the goods over time due to mean reversion. This is just one of the many examples of this debate that will endure as it has endured.

Yet what the debates neglect to mention is perhaps the most exciting part of our business—the markets really don't care. All participants will be humbled, many crushed. Mr. Market has no regard for hedge fund managers' viewpoints, pedigrees, upbringings, or educational degrees. So the PhD and the Nobel Prize winner can blow up their fund several times. A Hungarian refugee can run a fund successfully, making billions and billions of dollars over 43 years. To me, this is one of the most fantastic things about the markets—they don't care who you are, and they will reward and punish you for only how you think and act, not for your gender, skin color, or shoe size.

Just as a drop of water affects the ocean, every manager and investor affects the markets—that's all. Nothing more. Ultimately, the markets move in the most unexpected and unpredictable ways. Everyone at one point or another will get things really wrong. Don't believe me? Just examine all of the Fed economic forecasts going into the crisis, or how supposed legends in the industry stumbled in 2008 caught half-naked at low tide. Markets—and some of the people who invest in them—are brutal. As an investor in hedge funds, all you can do is make sure that you clearly define your investment objectives and have a disciplined process steeped in due diligence.

That being said, results matter and capital markets reward results. And naturally, assets are allocated to the investment vehicles, strategies, and firms that yield those best results. As an industry that grew leaps and bounds from 1999 to 2012, the hedge fund industry is one of those asset recipients. Thus, it will naturally continue to grow. Shoot flaming arrows, throw eggs and tomatoes,

get a few denouncements on the U.S. Senate floor—
and throw in a few haughty articles from a few envious
journalists—it doesn't matter. The industry will continue
to grow because of its ability to mitigate risk and generate returns regardless of market conditions. Sure, there
will be pauses and setbacks, but the industry is set to triple over the next decade. And guess what? A lot of people are going to get—and continue to get—rich in the
process.

It is an exciting time. It's an unnerving time. It won't
be perfect. There will be failures and setbacks and tumult
and surprises. But there will also be new innovations,
strategies, and products. As you read this *Little Book*,
there is an ambitious, talented, skilled, contrarian,
innovative, novice hedge fund manager who is doing this
right now. This person will become an industry titan
in the next decade and a half and further the evolution of
the industry.

If you are reading this and want to enter this field, go
back and re-read Chapter 10 on getting a job in the industry. Remember to be creative, be perseverant, and work
hard! Take your education very seriously. Focus on your
coursework and GPA. Hone your discipline so that when
someone looks at your resume, they see an accounting
Army Ranger or a finance Navy SEAL. Become disciplined. Proactive. Creative. Thoughtful. A calculated

risk taker. This will only happen through preparation and experience.

■ ■ ■

The fact remains: Life is full of uncertainty. Yet, in my humble opinion, the hedge fund industry will continue to grow, albeit in traditional and even unorthodox ways. Legendary managers, like Dave Tepper from Appaloosa, have given back money choosing to run their own and less of other peoples. It is quite possible that this strategy will be a trend for the future. As Yogi Berra did say, "The future isn't what it used to be." After all, no one can really predict it with any certainty.

Yet, there are a few things that will always be certain . . . many of which I urge you to take away with you:

1. **Have Passion**: Don't be in the hedge fund industry just for money; be a part of it because you have a passion for money management.

2. **Build Your Network**: You can never have enough business acquaintances or friends, many of whom will be the font of your best ideas.

3. **Read**: I don't just say this because I am an author; I say it because we are in a high-paced world and knowledge is power. Reading will keep you ahead of the curve.

4. **Ask Tons of Questions**: Make sure you are using every ounce of your intellectual curiosity. Don't get stuck or locked into rigid conventional thinking.

5. **Be Skeptical**: There is evil out there and it comes masked in many different faces, shapes, and forms. Make sure you are aware of it and keep your guard up.

6. **Exercise**: This sounds silly but it clears the mind and reduces stress. This industry is a synonym for stress. Exercise will allow you time to think clearly.

7. **Make Time for Yourself**: Sure you want to grow a business and sometimes you have to get away from it all. It will give you a better perspective.

8. **Don't Underestimate People**: People are smart. So, make sure you include thought leaders into your networking endeavours. Be accessible to people who are accessible to you. I know it's impossible to do that entirely, but at least ring fence a group of smart people and make sure you interact.

9. **Admit Mistakes and Keep Moving**: Be capable of admitting mistakes and correcting them quickly. The best traders are the best at this.

Lastly,

10. **Go Out of Your Way to Help Others**: That is the secret of all of the legends. Each of the ones who I know personally has made a ton of millionaires. You can start that process by unilaterally reaching out and helping your friends.

■ ■ ■

The bottom line is this: Hedge funds add value in a multitude of ways, many of which have been highlighted throughout this *Little Book of Hedge Funds*. As smart, passionate, hungry, articulate, and highly motivated people continue to flock to this industry, it will continue to grow at a surprising rate. The best thing you can do is be involved in this growth—be involved as an investor, benefactor of an institutional investor, employee (or parent of an employee), or industry member. Don't be afraid. Don't opt out. If you do, you will miss a great long-term return profile.

Hedge funds are affecting all of us and now you know a little bit from this Little Book about how and why.

Appendix

Due Diligence Questionnaire

~

I. Scope (what to assess)

A. Firm
   1. Firm ownership.
   2. Portfolio manager's investment in fund (i.e., does he have his own skin in the game?).
   3. Registrations with domestic and international regulatory agencies.
   4. History of legal/regulatory actions against firm or key people—conduct background checks.
   5. Firm-wide AUM history and composition.

6. Overall staffing adequacy and turnover history.

7. Employees related to each other or to employees of service providers.

B. Fund

1. Redemption terms (i.e., when an investor can get his money back).

2. Monthly net assets history.

3. Any NAV or performance restatements.

4. Investor concentrations.

5. Caliber of auditor, any qualifications or unusual notes in audit—visit and perform due diligence on any unknown auditors.

6. Independence and quality of offshore fund's board of directors.

7. Quality of fund's documents and caliber of law firm that drafted them.

8. Fund structure and any potential for cross-share class liability (i.e. if the liabilities of one share class exceed its assets, are investors in other share classes on the hook for the deficit?).

C. Operations

1. Qualifications of middle (e.g., COO) and back office (e.g., CFO) staff.

2. Segregation of duties between front office (trading and research) versus middle office (trade processing) and back office (accounting).

3. Any outsourcing of the mid-back office.

4. Front, mid, and back office systems, and access restrictions placed on these systems.

5. Controls on movement of cash.

6. Trade processing, reconciliation, and allocation.

7. Valuation, valuation, valuation—role of the portfolio manager versus the mid-back office, role of management firm versus the fund administrator; daily versus month-end procedures.

8. Prime brokers and custodians.

9. Counterparty risk and how it is being measured/tracked (e.g., Lehman Brothers default).

10. Fund administrator—self-administration/self-valuation by manager not acceptable.

D. Infrastructure

1. IT environment, use of third-party IT consultants.

2. Disaster Recovery (DR) and Continuity of Business (COB) Plan.

3. DR/COB testing frequency and availability of results.

E. Compliance

1. Formal compliance manual.

2. Compliance officer, use of third-party compliance consultant.

    3. Compliance testing frequency and availability of results.

    4. Specific policies and procedures, for example, personal trading, anti-money-laundering, transactions by the hedge fund with affiliates of the manager, potential conflicts of interest.

II. Process

A. Have manager complete a significant due diligence questionnaire (AIMA DDQ is industry standard).

B. Conduct on-site due diligence visit to:

    1. Interview the firm's principals, COO, CFO, compliance officer, IT head, and investor relations representative.

    2. Get a demonstration of front, mid, and back office systems.

    3. Inspect the firm's server room and determine its security.

    4. Tour the office and see how functions are segregated.

C. Conduct background investigations on the fund, the firm, its owners, and key persons.

D. Contact clearing brokers and custodians to independently confirm and verify relationship status, cash controls, any past issues.

E. Contact fund administrator to independently confirm and verify:
   1. Relationship status, any past issues.
   2. Services being provided (is administrator also providing mid-back office functions to manager?).
   3. Fund's monthly net assets history.
   4. Fund's monthly net performance history.
   5. Any NAV or performance restatements.
   6. Involvement in controls on movement of cash.
   7. Valuation procedures.
   8. Where the fund's assets are currently being custodied or otherwise held (e.g., margin posted to counterparties).
   9. Amount of hedge fund manager's investment in fund.
   10. Anti-money-laundering procedures.
F. Visit and due diligence for any unknown service providers, for example, auditor, clearing brokers, custodians, fund administrator, and/or mid-back office provider (if outsourced).
G. Complete a written analysis of the noninvestment risks to summarize and assess them.
H. Weigh these risks (along with the perceived investment-related risks) against the expected

return of the investment—what is the investor's tolerance for these risks?

I. Post investment, conduct regular monitoring and due diligence:

1. Monthly call with the manager to determine performance drivers, portfolio changes, summary risk information, and any significant changes with the firm or fund.

2. Formal weekly/monthly/quarterly risk reporting and monitoring of the investment.

3. Annual or more frequent formal due diligence to reassess business and operational risks, in addition to a formal repeat of the investment due diligence.

Notes

Introduction

1. Everett M. Ehrlich, "The Changing Role of Hedge Funds in the Global Economy," September 13, 2011, www.top1000funds .com/wp-content/uploads/2011/09/The-changing-role-of-hedge-funds-in-the-global-economy.pdf.

2. Robert A. Jaeger, *All About Hedge Funds* (New York: McGraw-Hill, 2003), 3–4.

3. Scott Frush, *Understanding Hedge Funds* (New York: McGraw-Hill, 2006).

4. Mark J. P. Anson, *The Handbook of Alternative Assets* (Hoboken, NJ: John Wiley & Sons, 2006), 123.

Chapter 1

1. David. F. Swensen. *Pioneering Portfolio Management: An Unconventional Approach to Institutional Investment* (Free Press, 2000).

Chapter 2

1. Tom Copeland and Vladimir Antikarov, *Real Options: A Practitioner's Guide* (New York: Texere, 2001).

2. Hugo Lindgre, "Long-Short Story Short," *New York Magazine*, April 9, 2007.

3. Sebastian Mallaby, *More Money Than God: Hedge Funds and the Making of a New Elite* (New York: The Penguin Press, 2010).

4. Daniel A. Strachman, *Getting Started in Hedge Funds*, 3rd ed. (Hoboken, NJ: John Wiley & Sons, 2011).

5. Michael Lewis, *The New New Thing: A Silicon Valley Story* (New York: W.W. Norton, 1999).

6. Gregory Zuckerman, *The Greatest Trade Ever: The Behind-the-Scenes Story of How John Paulson Defied Wall Street and Made Financial History* (New York: Crown Business, 2010).

Chapter 3

1. Carol Loomis, *Fortune*, January 1970, www.thehedgefundjournal .com/research/fortune/hard-times-come-to-the-hedge-funds-loomis-fortune-1-70.pdf.

2. Daniel A. Strachman, *Getting Started in Hedge Funds*, 3rd ed. (Hoboken, NJ: John Wiley & Sons, 2011).

3. This list has been taken from the SEC website at www.sec.gov/answers/accred.htm.

4. Steven Drobny, *Inside the House of Money: Top Hedge Fund Traders on Profiting in the Global Markets* (Hoboken, NJ: John Wiley & Sons, 2006).

5. Duff McDonald, "The Running of the Hedgehogs," *New York Magazine*, April 9, 2007, http://nymag.com/news/features/2007/hedgefunds/30341/index3.html.

6. 2011 Prequin Global Investment Report: Hedge Funds, www .preqin.com/docs/reports/Preqin_Global_Investor_Report_ Hedge_Funds.pdf.

7. Everett M. Ehrlich, "The Changing Role of Hedge Funds in the Global Economy," September 13, 2011, www.top1000funds .com/wp-content/uploads/2011/09/The-changing-role-of-hedge-funds-in-the-global-economy.pdf.

8. Ibid.

9. McDonald, "The Running of the Hedgehogs."

10. Ehrlich, "The Changing Role of Hedge Funds in the Global Economy."

11. Ibid.

Chapter 4

1. McDonald, "The Running of the Hedgehods."

2. Stephanie Strom, "Top Manager to Close Shop on Hedge Funds," *New York Times*, October 12, 1995, www.nytimes .com/1995/10/12/business/top-manager-to-close-shop-on-hedge-funds.html?pagewanted=all&src=pm.

Chapter 6

1. Andrei Shleifer and Lawrence Summers, "The Noise Trader Approach to Finance," Journal of Economic Perspectives 4, no. 2 (Spring 1990), www.economics.harvard.edu/faculty/shleifer/ files/noise_trader_approach_finance.pdf.

Chapter 7

1. Sebastian Mallaby, *More Money Than God: Hedge Funds and the Making of a New Elite* (New York: Penguin Press, 2010).

2. Jennifer Karchmer, "Tiger Management Closes," March 30, 2000, http://money.cnn.com/2000/03/30/mutualfunds/q_funds_tiger/.

3. Filippo Stefanini, *Investment Strategies of Hedge Funds* (Hoboken, NJ: John Wiley & Sons, 2006).

4. Ibid.

Chapter 9

1. Scott P. Frush. *Financial Times*.

Chapter 10

1. Bethany McLean, "Everybody's Going Hedge Funds," *Fortune,* June 8, 1998, http://money.cnn.com/magazines/fortune/fortune_archive/1998/06/08/243511/.

2. Steve Fishman, "Get Richest Quickest," *New York Magazine,* May 21, 2005.

3. Michael Steinhardt, *No Bull: My Life In and Out of Markets* (New York: John Wiley & Sons, 2001).

Acknowledgments

This book would have been impossible to write without the tireless energy and passionate commitment of Kelly O'Connor. In addition to providing excellent research, editorial direction and relevant content, she did a fantastic job of helping me find my voice on these topics. She has a great writing style and is a true storyteller. She also did a great job of keeping this project afloat while I juggled a lot of different responsibilities as Managing Partner of SkyBridge Capital.

The SkyBridge Capital Team also provided a tremendous amount of content, support, and firsthand accounts. In particular, Ray Nolte, Co-Managing Partner and Chief Investment Officer, and Troy Gayeski, Senior Portfolio

Manager were instrumental in providing commentary on the fund of hedge fund business, manager selection, portfolio composition, and trade insights. In addition to being great business partners, they are exceptional guys and make each and every working day of my life a lot easier. Victor Oviedo, the George Washington of the SALT Conference, read the text, provided ideas, and helped us access our friends in the industry. Ken McDonald, Managing Director, did a magnificent job of adding content on due diligence and manager selection—he is a living example of what to do right from a diligence perspective. Peter Stern, Senior Vice-President, provided us with valuable insight on value investing and stock selection—at his core he is a true value investor and someone I would trust to manage and execute my trades. Max von Bismarck, Robert Duggan, Michael Gubenko and Jon McEvoy also proved to be valuable resources as they were always available to discuss current trends and make editorial suggestions. I'd also like to thank some other folks at SkyBridge: Deidre Ball, Marie Noble, Amanda Ober, Sue Ponce, Joe Rosano, and Jason Wright (whose young daughter Evangeline is the most courageous and spirited of us all).

We are grateful at SkyBridge for having great friends and partners in the hedge fund business. Steven A. Cohen, Robert Matza, Leon Cooperman, Barton M. Biggs, Lee Ainslie, Steve Tanabaum, Steve Kuhn, Theo Phanoes,

Deepak Narula, John Burbank, Andrew K. Boszhardt Jr., Dan Loeb, Paul Singer, Cliff Asness, Izzy Englander, Jamie Dinan, Russ Bernard, Ken Griffin and many others. We are also pride ourselves in being students of Nouriel Roubini, David M. Darst, Michael Milken, Ed Mathias, David Rubenstein, William Conway, Dan D'Aniello, Prof. Josh Shapiro, Woody Brock, Frank Meyer, and Oliver Stone.

My friends at CNBC have been nothing short of amazing. Susan Krakower, Mark Hoffman, Nik Deogun, Melissa Lee, Scott Wapner, Mary Duffy, John Melloy, Patty Martell, Lydia Thew, Gary Kaminsky, Maria Bartiromo, David Faber, Guy Adami, Joe Terranova, Tim Seymour, Amanda Drury, Carl Quintanilla, Jim Cramer, Brian Steel, Brian Sullivan, Maneet Ahuja, Pete and Jon Najarian, Steve Grasso, Steve Cortes, Karen Finerman, Brian Sullivan, Samantha Wright, and a legion of others who always make my time on the network a great learning experience.

I also want to acknowledge my brother David; my sister Susan; my mom and dad, Al and Marie Scaramucci; the mother of my children, Lisa; and if you read my first book *Goodbye Gordon Gekko,* my first business mentor Uncle Salvatore Defeo, Sonny, Bobby, and Augie Defeo. If I have left anyone out, I offer an apology. The oversight, while unintentional, is more of a function of a publishing deadline and a warning by my publisher not to make this too long.